AF865950

JAMES W. LAMPREY

Boomers vs Millennials

Who Really Had It Easier to Buy A House?

First published by Finance Understood 2026

Copyright © 2026 by James W. Lamprey

All rights reserved. No part of this publication may be reproduced, stored, or transmitted in any form or by any means, electronic, mechanical, photocopying, recording, scanning, or otherwise without written permission from the publisher. It is illegal to copy this book, post it to a website, or distribute it by any other means without permission.

James W. Lamprey asserts the moral right to be identified as the author of this work.

James W. Lamprey has no responsibility for the persistence or accuracy of URLs for external or third-party Internet Websites referred to in this publication and does not guarantee that any content on such Websites is, or will remain, accurate or appropriate.

Designations used by companies to distinguish their products are often claimed as trademarks. All brand names and product names used in this book and on its cover are trade names, service marks, trademarks, and registered trademarks of their respective owners. The publishers and the book are not associated with any product or vendor mentioned in this book. None of the companies referenced within the book have endorsed the book.

First edition

ISBN (paperback): 979-8-9976630-0-1
ISBN (hardcover): 979-8-9976630-1-8

This book was professionally typeset on Reedsy.
Find out more at reedsy.com

Contents

Introduction

The great housing affordability debate! You would have to be hiding under a rock if you haven't seen or heard someone mention how housing is unaffordable today. The debate seems endless. People are passionate about why they believe housing is so expensive and there is no greater generational divide than that between Boomers and Millennials. Other generations have escaped the cross hairs for now but I'm sure that is just a temporary situation.

We've all overheard our Boomer uncle at a holiday dinner tell your Millennial cousin that he just needs to save more and work harder while your cousin snaps back with a mention of how houses don't cost $35,000 anymore and that the Boomer uncle didn't need to take on crippling student debt. Both are telling the truth. But both are also leaving out a lot of important information.

This book is an attempt to replace unfounded or half-truths about homeownership affordability using a data-driven approach. We are going to dive deep into the data to help us explain what that "inexpensive" Boomer house would actually cost today. Does that house look so inexpensive after we adjust for inflation, wages, interest rates, house size, and a full gamut of important factors?

The central argument around homeownership affordability is not that things were easy then or hard now. The question itself is the problem. Comparing housing across generations almost always relies on raw numbers, selective memory and emotional narratives that obscure more than they reveal. Taking the emotion out of this argument and looking closely at the data for things like CPI adjustments, debt-to-income ratios, price-per-square-foot calculations and an honest look at both era's burdens. This reveals a more complicated and frankly a more interesting story.

Throughout this book I want to challenge each of you to put aside your own judgments, be open to discovering different perspectives and find the courage to look more clearly at the data to answer the ultimate question of "Who had it easier to buy a house, Boomers or Millennials?"

1

Chapter 1- Did Boomers Really Have It Easy?

The baby boomer generation lived in a time like no other. Called the baby boomer generation because their parents returned home from fighting in World War II and quickly got to work starting a family. The birth rate in the United States skyrocketed during this time. As they grew up and were coming of age, the interstate highway system was well underway. The highway system opened up access to distant undeveloped land. Permits were easy to get and regulations were minimal. Home developers started building cookie-cutter homes as fast as they could get the materials delivered. A new age of possibilities opened up for this generation.

Enticed by the opportunity to have something they could call their own, Boomers ventured out of cities to the suburbs to seek the American Dream. This wasn't an easy decision for many of them. The thought of a long daily commute to and from work might have been a negative but it was a sacrifice many made to own a home. Prior to the expansion of the highway system, people generally lived where they worked. Cities offered easy transportation options and close proximity to not only work but other resources like grocery stores and other necessities. The highway system opened up new possibilities that just didn't exist before.

The consistent narrative around Boomer's is that they had it easy. Many would say they were fortunate to have lived through a time that showered them with opportunities that no other generation was offered. They came of age after World War II, they enjoyed the economic boom of post-war spending (both by governments and individuals) and low prices. But are these facts or just perceptions?

Now let's explore the narrative around Millennials. It's a common stance that Millennials are drowning in student loan debt. They are unable to find affordable housing because those houses do not exist anymore. Many of them are frustrated with their outlook on life as they compare their situations to where their parents or grandparents were in the same stages of life.

It is true that more Americans are going to college today than have ever gone in the past. In 1975 only about 14% of adults 25 or older had college degrees while in 2025 that number was nearly 50%. There are many reasons for this. The US moving from an industrialized country to a service based country, government subsidized loans which has driven education costs through the roof and technical jobs requiring advanced skills.

Many Millennials feel they need to go to college to have a good career. They don't want to take out loans but feel as though they will be left behind professionally if they don't.

Millennials have lived through a time where they have seen one of the largest spikes in inflation this country has experienced in the last 40 years. The June of 2022 peak of 9.1% was hard for everyone but especially hard for those who didn't own assets like real estate. For them, the American dream of owning a home with a white picket fence and a big backyard seems like a pipedream and for many of them, it still is.

Both of these narratives contain real truth, however neither contains the whole truth. The gap between these two narratives has become one of the most contentious, most emotionality charged debates. And lets not forget, the most analytically inaccurate debates in modern times.

Why Headlines Oversimplify

The media coverage on this debate follows a predictable formula. They start with an old 1975 advertisement showing a house for sale with the $30,000 price front and centered. Their producers know that this will generate a great deal of outrage and engagement from their young audiences. A quick glance at the post shows this incredibly low nominal price and when comparing that price to the typical prices of houses today seems incredibly cheap. The comment sections filled with affirmation about this confirms that Boomers had it easy. The post did its job, it created emotional engagement that will push this post in the algorithms and possibly be picked up by other news agencies and maybe even a national news desk.

At the same time, social media influencers are picking up this story and sharing it with their audiences. The comment sections are filled immediately with two camps of people:

Those who insist it's proof that Boomers had it easy, and those who insist inflation makes the comparison meaningless. Both are half right.

One of the many things these headlines will not include is that mortgage rates in 1975 were around 9%. By 1981 it reached 16.6% The difference in monthly payments on a $30,000 house at 9% ($241/month) vs 16.6% ($418/month) jumped 73% in just a few years. While mortgage rates in 2025 were under 7%.

When comparing arguments, it is just as important to understand what was not shown as well as to what was shown. As I examined this debate in detail, I found a lot of data that was cherry picked to emphasize the narrative of whoever was telling the story. Most of this debate is around nominal prices without factoring in inflation or they are comparing "average" numbers to "median" numbers.

Confirmation Bias

Throughout this book I will explore housing affordability from the lens of Boomers, Millennials and other generations. There will be many different variables needed to be looked at for accurate comparisons. Often, people will jump on the first set of data points that seems to confirm their notions about this topic. In a complex debate such as this, it's important to review all the data before coming to a conclusion.

As humans, we all have confirmation bias. The challenge is to understand this as we gather and analyze the data. It took me many months of writing and rewriting this book to be sure that I didn't let my own confirmation bias get in the way of a true comparative analysis.

While many of us understand that our confirmation bias will influence our decisions to pick certain data points to emphasize, a lot of people online will not. If you haven't noticed it yet, you will from this moment on. You will see posts where people compare nominal prices without mentioning inflation-adjusted prices, average houses compared to median houses and so on.

The Internet's Favorite Sport: Cherry-Picking Data

If you spend enough time online, you will quickly notice that housing debates often resemble political debates rather than economic analysis. People search for the statistic that supports their existing position and then stop looking.

You will see someone post a chart showing that homes were three times household income in the 1970s and nearly five times household income today. Another person responds with a chart showing mortgage rates were 9% in 1975 and over 16% in 1981. Someone else points out that homes today are much larger than they were fifty years ago. Another person argues that student debt barely existed for most Boomers.

Everyone is sharing data. Few people are sharing all the data.

This isn't always because people are trying to be dishonest. Most of the time it's because people tend to seek out information that confirms their own experiences. If you bought a home in 1978, you'll remember skyrocketing mortgage payments due to high interest rates. If you are buying your first home in 2025, you'll remember sticker shock at those prices.

Both are valid experiences.

The problem is when we start to believe our experiences are the same as everyone's experiences.

Are You Comparing Apples to Oranges?

A similar type of confirmation bias is when we compare apples to oranges. Housing markets present us with enormous data points that we can interpret incorrectly. More data, more opportunities to fall into this trap.

Examples include:

- **Comparative Sizes** - Comparing a 1,550-square foot home from 1975 to a 2,300-square foot home in 2025.
- **Starter-home fallacy** - Comparing a starter home in one generation to the "average" home in another.
- **Geographical bias** - Comparing home prices in rural America in the 1970s to home prices in major coastal cities today.
- **Boom-bust bias** - Comparing one generation's best-case scenario to the other generation's average experience.

Each of these arguments can create sensational headlines and social media posts. But they rarely get us closer to the truth. If we want to talk about home affordability honestly, we must try to compare apples to apples wherever possible.

Why experience can trick your mind

Part of the reason why the housing debate gets so heated is because people use their own life as anecdotal evidence. "I bought a home at age 25 so why can't they?" "I've been saving for years with no luck. Buying a home must be impossible!"

Neither statement is definitively proven by looking at the data.

We naturally take what we have experienced and apply it to everyone. The problem is just because your story happened, doesn't mean everyone's story did too. The housing market your parents experienced in Pittsburgh was probably very different from the one their friends experienced in San Diego.

The housing market in 1975 looked very different from the housing market just a few years later in 1981. The experience for two people born in the exact same year can dramatically differ based on circumstances.

Recognizing Confirmation Bias

When I started researching and writing this book I realized I was prone to these biases as much as anyone else. In fact, several times I had to stop and question my own assumptions. I uncovered data that countered conclusions I had previously reached. I had to rewrite entire chapters because the context had changed as I learned more. I found clever arguments that made sense until I dug deeper and found more data.

That was part of the frustration of writing this book. But it was also why it needed to be written.

I don't want this book to tell you that Boomers had it better. I don't want this book to tell you that Millennials have it worse. I want this book to show you what actually happened. And to do that I, and you, need to be willing to follow the data, even when it leads us to conclusions we don't like.

A Note to My Readers

I want you to keep an open mind as you read the following chapters. When you read something that confirms your existing beliefs, resist the impulse to share that article or translate that into a Facebook post. Challenge yourself instead.

Ask yourself:

- "What information would disprove my belief?"
- "Am I cherry picking one data point and ignoring others?"
- "Am I comparing apples to apples?"
- "Am I trusting my personal experience more than the data?"

But most of all, know this. Housing affordability is not a black and white issue. It's not easy to parse through emotionally charged debates and try to find objective truths. But it can be done.

Boomers could have benefited from lower home price-to-income ratios AND paid higher mortgage rates. Millennials could have larger homes with modern amenities while also dealing with higher prices and student loans.

It's possible for both sides to be right... and wrong.

This book isn't here to prove which generation is correct. It's here to explain why they both believe they are. Understanding starts with recognizing the bias we are all guilty of... seeing what we want to see.

2

Chapter 2 - How to Compare Two Different Worlds

The biggest problem with most comparisons on housing affordability data is not that they are using wrong numbers, it is that the numbers they are using don't tell the whole story. The viral post showing a 1975 house priced at $30,000 is factually accurate. The quick responses about inflation are also accurate. But both miss the point! We need to find out if the comparison is meaningful and what other factors may be at play here.

Comparing housing affordability across fifty years requires more than simply adjusting for inflation. It requires finding a common denominator for each variable. This might be fairly easy to do with inflation but not all variables can be quantified using a historical data calculator.

This chapter establishes the framework that will guide my analysis. Without this framework it would be easy to find ourselves exploring non-relevant information and leaving out important information. It is not the most exciting chapter but it's certainly the most important. Without this framework it would be easy to find one data point or one metric and use that to perpetuate a narrative. Understanding that confirmation bias is a big reason why this debate has sparked so many emotions.

The Five Variables That Actually Matter

If we are going to have a serious discussion about housing affordability across different decades we must account for at least five core variables. Leave out any of these variables and your comparison is not just wrong, it is dead wrong!

It's not just comparing apples to oranges but instead comparing apples to couch.

Variable 1: Nominal Price (The Headline Number)

This is the number everyone sees first. It's the price of the home in the dollars of that year. In 1975, the median price of a house in the US sold for $39,300. This number might look exceptionally low looking at it through the lens of someone today. But at the time, $39,300 was a lot of money. In 2025, the median price was $416,000. This increase of more than 10 times in price is the fundamental basis of every "Boomers had it easy" argument.

The nominal price matters because this is what buyers actually have to write a check for at the time of the sale. In 1975 a buyer needed to produce $39,300 or finance a large part of it. This was no easy task considering the median household salary was only $11,800 a year. A buyer in 2025 needed to produce $416,000. That is a significantly larger number than the $39,300 a Boomer had to produce to purchase their house. There is something to be said for the psychological weight of those two numbers.

But focusing on nominal price alone is useless for comparison because it ignores the changing value of money. A dollar in 1975 could buy far more things than a dollar in 2025. Comparing $39,000 in 1975 to $416,000 in 2025 is like comparing temperatures on different scales and concluding that 25 degrees is colder than 77 degrees. But you did this without first understanding that the 25 degree temperature was listed in Celsius while the 77 degree temperature was listed in Fahrenheit. This would be completely wrong and it highlights the importance of not just citing data but also understanding it.

Variable 2: Inflation Adjustment

One of the best tools we have for calculating inflation comes from the U.S. Bureau of Labor Statistics (BLS). The BLS has a handy inflation calculator on their website. This measures the Consumer Price Index (CPI). CPI measures the changing cost of a "basket of goods" and services over time. The CPI measures hundreds of thousands of goods and services that an average household buys every year. There are eight major categories of products included in the CPI data. These are:

- Housing - this measures just about everything involving shelter. Things like rent, utilities and home furnishings.
- Transportation - this category measures the costs of new and used vehicles, gasoline and even public transportation.
- Food and Beverages - this measures groceries, dining out and alcohol.
- Medical Care - this category includes health insurance, medical services and prescription costs.
- Recreation - this category measures admission costs, sports equipment, televisions and oddly enough, pets.
- Education and communication - this includes tuition, phones, internet services and childcare expenses.
- Apparel - includes stuff like clothing, footwear and jewelry.
- Other goods and services - includes haircuts, personal care products and tobacco products.

Keep in mind that the CPI calculator is not perfect. It has many limitations especially when it tries to capture product improvements, substitutions and regional variations. Still, it is the best tool we have.

The U.S. Bureau of Labor Statistics (BLS) has methods of adjusting for product improvements when it calculates inflation. How they do this will depend on what the specific product is. As an example, if a bicycle they measured in the past used to use aluminum for its frame and they switched to a stronger composite material, the BLS would use the "direct cost adjustment" to determine how much of the price difference is due to inflation versus the added cost of the new material. The BLS uses different methods for different types of products. They may use the Hedonic Quality Adjustment for more complex products like vehicles and cell phones.

The BLS does a great job trying to give us the most accurate information about inflation. Regardless of the method they use, it is impossible to have a perfect comparison every time. I used the BLS's CPI calculator numerous times during my analysis.

When we plug in the 1975 median house price of $39,300 into the CPI calculator, we get about a price of $236,500 in 2025 dollars. This is what a 1975 house would cost if it had appreciated only at the rate of inflation.

The gap between $236,500 (inflation-only) and $416,000 (actual 2025 price) is the real price appreciation: about 1.76x. This represents the price increase that cannot be explained from the dollar losing value (inflation). It means there are other factors to consider.

There is a key psychological distinction between saying a house is 10x (nominal price) more expensive today than in 1975 and saying a house is 1.76x (inflation-only price) more expensive today than in 1975. Those who don't understand how inflation works will argue simply that house prices are 10 times more in 2025 than they used to be in 1975.

When I was growing up, I was one of those people who didn't understand inflation. Thinking back to my own childhood being a GenX kid who was born in the mid-1970s and growing up in the 1980s, I remember the hardships that so many people have seemed to have forgotten.

In the mid 80s I was watching a movie with my parents. It was an Elvis movie filmed many years earlier. In this movie Elvis purchased a new Cadillac automobile for around $4,000. Me being young and unaware of how inflation worked said to my father "why didn't you buy a bunch of new Cadillac's when you were younger?" I knew a Cadillac at the time of watching this movie in the mid 1980s was selling for around $20,000 but until watching that movie it never crossed my mind how the same product could cost so much less in a different era.

This was the moment my parents began to educate me about inflation.

In my young, naive state I didn't realize that inflation had such an impact on incomes and prices of goods. Without real life experience I couldn't understand how prices could change so much over time.

This single experience from my childhood helped shape my thirst for knowledge about economics and finance. After seeing many younger generations focus their blame on Boomers and Generation X, I decided to break down the numbers in a true apples-to-apples comparison.

While data alone won't help the affordability of younger generations, I hope it will bring a better understanding. With this new understanding, more effective plans can be made to solve these complicated issues.

Variable 3: Mortgage Interest Rates (The Forgotten Cost)

Now here is where most comparisons fall apart. Interest rates are a significant factor in determining affordability on a monthly basis. Most people do not pay cash for their homes and loans are needed. On average only about 8% of first-time homebuyers pay all cash for a purchased house. This means that for 92% of them, interest rates matter. Borrowing costs can negatively affect affordability in a dramatic way.

Let's look at an example of how much interest rates can affect monthly payments using real numbers:

The following chart shows a $100,000 loan amount at 4 different times in American history. From the historic low rates of 2021 to the all time highs of 1981.

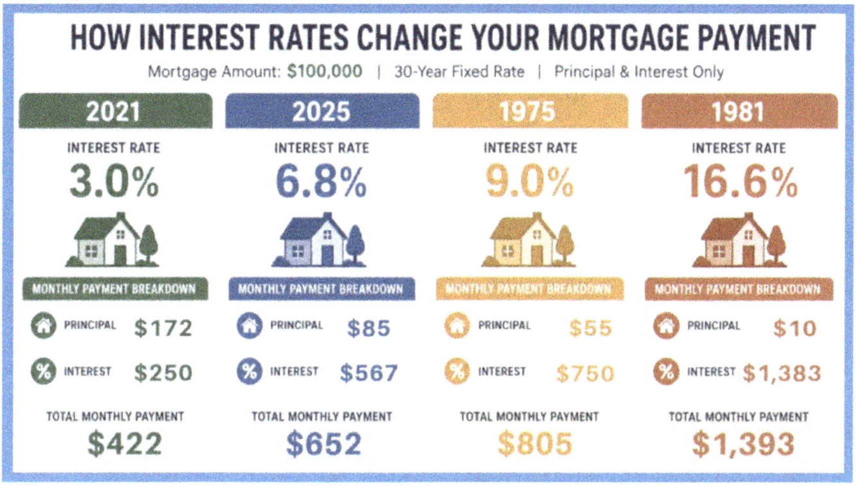

Sources: Federal Reserve Bank of St. Louis and Freddie Mac

That same $100,000 loan in 1981 costs more than 3x as much at 16.6% as it would have cost at 3%. In addition to all that extra interest, homeowners with higher interest rates pay less each month towards the principle of the house. Shown in the example above, a borrower in 1975 would only pay $55 a month towards the principal of their loan while a borrower in 2025 would pay $85 a month towards the principal. Not as drastic of a difference from 1981 to 2021 but still significant. Interest rates play a huge role in determining affordability. Any comparison that ignores interest rates is not a true comparison at all.

Variable 4: Household Income

To determine if a house is affordable or not, there is a very important factor we must consider. That is income, specifically household income. We use household income because that is the true test of affordability. I have seen many arguments comparing household incomes to individual incomes. This is not a true comparison. While this might be obvious, it gets overlooked in almost every comparison.

In 1975, median household annual income was $11,800. That's less than $1,000 a month. In 2025, it was $83,700 or almost $7,000 a month. A nominal increase of over 7x and a 1.18x (real) inflation adjusted increase.

The price-to-income ratio is a very important metric to compare affordability.

1975

$39,800 house ÷$11,800 income = **3.37**

2025

$416,000 house ÷$83,700 income = **4.97**

This metric shows how much of your income is required to purchase a house outright. In 2025, to buy a median house while making a median income, Millennials will need about 5x their annual income. Boomers on the other hand only needed a little over 3x their annual income.

But just like any other single metric, this alone can't be used to conclude who had it easier. That will take some more analyzing.

It is important to understand that these two numbers are not equally comparable. Household income measures all occupants in a house 15 or older. In 1975, most households were single-earner households. In 2025, more households were multiple-earner households.

Recognizing the difference between a single-earner household and a multiple-earner household matters. This represents a structural change in purchasing power.

Variable 5: Size and Quality

The fifth variable is one that almost never gets its due in social media debates but it needs to be understood to have an honest debate. That is the realization that house sizes between 1975 and 2025 were different.

While researching for this book, this information seemed to be the most difficult to acquire. To be clear, I found lots of information about "average" square footage of houses throughout the decades and I found median square footage of "newly constructed" houses but the most difficult data to find was data on the median square footage of all houses sold in those years.

The US Census started to collect median square footage of "Newly" constructed houses in 1973. The problem with this data is that it doesn't tell us anything about the houses built prior to 1973 that were sold in 1975. Now why would we need this information if we are only comparing houses from 1975 to 2025.

Most people purchase existing houses, not newly built homes. To get accurate data we need to examine sales of both newly built houses and pre-existing houses. The US Census did report in its "How American Homes Vary By The Year They Were Built" working paper published in June of 2011 that "The median square footage of a single-family home built in the 1960s or earlier stands at 1,500 square feet today." But this did not specifically break down home sales.

While we might know the square footage of a house when it was built, we don't know how many of those houses added square footage over the years. To get an accurate picture of square footage of preexisting houses we are missing a few years of data from a reliable source such as the US Census. Almost every source I could find lists average square footage for those years. Because averages can be skewed by outliers we have to realize that these numbers are not the best to use for analysis.

In 1975, a median newly constructed home was approximately 1,550 square feet, it lacked central air conditioning, came with small, no-frills kitchens, single-pane windows, basic electrical wiring (100-amp), small bedrooms and unfinished basements. These houses were functional but they were definitely not luxurious. Some would describe these houses as a box with four walls and a roof.

The median size of both existing homes and newly constructed homes combined sold in 1975 was about 1,500 square feet.

In 2025, a median newly constructed home was approximately 2,300 square feet, it was about 48% larger, central heating and air conditioning, modern kitchen with granite or quartz counter tops, stainless steel appliances, double or triple-pane windows, 200-amp electrical systems and most of the time a finished basement. Energy-efficient HVAC and many other features that simply did not exist in 1975. These houses are not just functional, they are equipped with modern day luxuries that those in 1975, as first-time homebuyers would only dream of.

The typical single-family home purchased in 2025 was roughly 1,950 square feet.. Because the vast majority of home purchases involve existing homes rather than new construction, these figures better reflect what buyers actually purchased than statistics based solely on new homes.

The National Association of Realtors "2025 Profile of Homebuyers and Sellers" report says the median of all single family homes sold was 1,900 square feet but this report included condos and mobile homes. Since most single family detached homes are typically larger than condos and mobile homes it's reasonable to assume that the median square footage of a detached home is larger than this figure.

To get a more accurate median square footage size I used this 1,900 sq ft figure times the percentage of existing single family homes sold and the 2,280 sq ft (2,300 sq ft approximation) size times the percentage of newly built homes to come to this estimate.

Here's the math:

(84%×1,900 sq ft)+(16%×2,280 sq ft)

=1,596+364.8

1,960.8 sq ft (1,950 sq ft approximation used throughout this book)

Something that is often forgotten in this debate is that these two houses (the one from 1975 and the one from 2025) are not the same house. These are two completely different products.

Comparing a median house in 1975 to a median house in 2025 is like comparing a horse and buggy to a Cadillac Escalade. They are both modes of transportation, they both have wheels and they both get you from point "A" to point "B" but that is about the extent of their similarities.

When we factor in home size in our calculations this narrows the price differential gap. Using a common denominator like square footage we are able to more accurately compare two different houses of different sizes.

In 1975, a $39,300 house ÷1,500 sq ft = $26.20 per sq ft

$26.20 in 1975 adjusted for inflation is $157.6

If we take the inflation adjusted price per square foot and multiply it by 2025's actual square footage of 1,950 we will get $307,457 which is a comparable price that factors in size and inflation but no other factors. This brings us a lot closer to the 2025 median price of $416,000.

There are no official historical reports measuring the median square footage of every single-family home sold, including both new and existing properties. However, combining Census data for new construction with estimates of the existing-home market suggests that the typical single-family home purchased in 1975 was approximately 1,500 square feet. By 2025, the comparable approximation was 1,950 square feet. New homes alone grew much more dramatically, but because existing homes represent most transactions, the increase for the overall sales market was smaller.

Average Price vs Median Price

Another problem that comes up regularly in the great home affordability debate is when people use averages instead of medians for data analysis.

Averages can be skewed by outliers. For instance, if 10 people are in a room and we are determining the average net worth where 4 of them have a net worth of $100,000, 2 have a $150,000 net worth, 3 have a net worth of $300,000 and 1 has a net worth of $5 million. The average net worth would be $660,000 per person. This is not an accurate representation of the group. Only one of them has a net worth of more than that amount and all the others are nowhere close to that net worth. This is why median is a more superior statistic.

Using the same example we used above to find the average, let's find the median. The median is simply the number in the middle. Half the people are worth more than the median and half the people are worth less than the median. Our median in this case would be $150,000 which is a better representation of actual net worth.

Throughout this book, we will use median figures whenever possible. This will help us more accurately analyze the data.

3

Chapter 3 - Sticker Price Shock of Nominal Prices

Year	Nominal Price	Inflation-Adjusted (2025 $)
1975	$39,300	$236,505
1985	$82,800	$245,100
1995	$130,000	$270,100
2005	$232,500	$380,800
2015	$289,200	$386,500
2025	$416,000	$416,000

Sources: U.S. Housing of Urban Development, U.S Census Bureau, U.S. Bureau of

Labor & Statistics

The number that is responsible for a large amount of arguments around housing affordability is the nominal price. We will call this the sticker price shock. This is the out of pocket dollar amount paid for a house in their respective years listed on the chart.

The Illusion of Raw Dollar Comparisons

The gap between home prices, even inflation-adjusted prices is real. Overall, home prices have outpaced inflation over the past 50 years. The question is not whether homes cost more today in real (nominal) terms, they do! But whether they are harder to purchase when you account for income, interest rates, size and amenities. Those are the questions we will address in the following chapters.

Over the last few years we have seen asset prices rise significantly. This is because in periods of high inflation, asset prices tend to rise fast. Those Millennials who were fortunate enough to purchase a house just a few years ago have benefited from their assets (houses) appreciating in value quickly. Unfortunately, those who were not able to purchase a home at that time missed out in some of the fastest appreciating years.

In contrast, those Boomers who bought their first house in the 20-year period between 1975 and 1995 only saw a total of a 20% increase of about 1% a year inflation adjusted. They did not get rich on price appreciation alone.

Talk to any Millennial today who has not purchased their first house yet and they would happily take a modest price appreciation instead of being faced with the reality of being priced out of the market completely.

There are many reasons why we find the housing market in this position. We can't ignore the physiological impacts of high nominal prices. Even when you factor in inflation adjustments, it's natural to be overwhelmed by the sticker shock of high prices. We are all human.

High house prices are not the only cost that has been affected by inflation. All the things that go into those homes have also risen in price year-after-year.

Things like building materials (wood, concrete and metal), appliances and windows to name a few.

We also can't overlook the land these houses sit on. As the population grows and houses get bigger, the amount of land required to build a house also increases. This goes into the total cost of a house.

Down Payment Shock

Do Homebuyers have to put 20% down on a home?

The simple answer is no.

In fact, only 6% to 9% of first time homebuyers actually put at least 20% down when purchasing a home. Although it is unusual for first time homebuyers to put down at least 20%, homebuyers who are purchasing their second or third property are far more likely to do so.

I think the reason so many people believe you "must" put a 20% down payment on a home is due to so many examples using that in their projections. As I write this book, I am no different. You will see this down payment example throughout this book because it's a common example used in various places and I want to keep it consistent so everyone can easily compare my analysis with a side-by-side analysis from elsewhere.

So why do people always seem to use a 20% down payment as the standard? The main reason for this is because 20% is the minimum down payment to avoid PMI (Private Mortgage Insurance) premiums. Why would you want to avoid PMI? Simple, PMI is expensive!

Private Mortgage Insurance PMI

What exactly is PMI?

PMI stands for Private Mortgage Insurance and most lenders require borrowers to have (and pay for) PMI if they have a Loan-to-Value (LTV) ratio of more than 80%.

Example would be if a homebuyer only put a 10% down payment on a home. Their LTV would be 90%.

If a lender requires PMI, the homebuyer is the one who has to pay the monthly premiums. This can be very costly and reduce the total affordability of a home. These premiums can amount to hundreds of dollars a month. That is hundreds of dollars not going to the principle of a mortgage for the homebuyer.

Even though it is the homebuyer who pays for this insurance, the benefit is not for the homebuyer. This insurance mitigates the losses of the lender if the homebuyer is foreclosed on. Some people will argue that the homebuyer benefits from getting a loan with less than a 20% down payment.

Let's look at what happens if a homebuyer defaults on their mortgage with PMI:

- First, the home goes into foreclosure proceedings
- The home goes to auction
- PMI insurance company pays the lender an agreed upon amount if there is a shortcoming from the sale at auction
- If there is a shortcoming at auction, the homeowner is still liable to repay the lender
- The homeowner's credit score is negatively affected.

When a defaulted mortgage goes into foreclosure the process differs from state-to-state but ultimately the home will end up going to auction. These auctions go to the highest bidder. Sometimes homes do not sell for typical market rates for the specific area where this home is located. This means that a home which has a $400,000 loan balance might sell at auction for only $300,000.

This creates a shortcoming of $100,000. The auctioneer will take any owed taxes if applicable and any fees then satisfy the lender's lien. It is at this point the lender will file a claim with the PMI insurer to recover their losses. Depending on the policy agreement, sometimes this does not satisfy the full $100,000 loss. Some lenders will bid on homes in these auctions to insure the house does not sell for too low of a price.

For the homeowner who was foreclosed this process is exceptionally hard on them. They lost their home, their credit score will be negatively affected for many years and they are still liable for the full amount of the loan.

Cost of PMI

How is PMI calculated?

PMI takes a lot of different factors into consideration to determine the amount a homebuyer will pay. They use loan amount, down payment percentage and credit scores to find your PMI rate. A homebuyer with a high credit score may only have a PMI rate of 0.3 while one with a lower credit score may have one for 1.5.

Using our median home price example of $416,000 from 2025 lets show how PMI would be calculated and how it would add to the monthly costs using different variables.

Scenario 1:

In this scenario we will assume a 10% down payment on a median home price of $416,000 which is $41,600. The PMI rate we are using for this example is 1.0 percent.

Monthly PMI = (Loan Amount x PMI percentage) \div 12

Here's the math for a 10% down payment:

Loan amount

- $416,000 - $41,600 (down payment) = $374,400 Loan amount

PMI

- $374,400 x 0.01 = $3,744/year
- $3,744 \div 12 = $312/month

One of the largest obstacles first-time homebuyers face in buying a home is a large down payment. Most first-time homebuyers do not put down the recommended 20% down payment on their first home.

This means that most of them will have to pay PMI. Monthly PMI payments reduce the amount of a home that the homebuyer can qualify for.

There are two main reasons this reduces the amount a homebuyer can qualify for:

Looking at the previous example, the loan amount of a $416,000 home with a 10% down payment is $374,400 versus a loan amount of $332,800 if the homebuyer puts in a 20% down payment. The smaller down payment results in more of the home needing to be financed.

The additional monthly cost is not just the PMI premiums, it is also the additional mortgage interest on the extra $41,600 being financed. That means it's not just $312 more a month but $585 more a month. That's a significant obstacle. In the next chapter I will explain more on how this and other variables affect debt-to-income ratios and ultimately the total price of a house someone can afford.

Scenario 2:

In this scenario we will assume a 5% down payment on a median home price of $416,000 which is $20,800. The PMI rate we are using for this example is 1.0 percent.

Monthly PMI = (Loan Amount x PMI percentage) \div 12

Here's the math for a 5% down payment:

- Loan amount
- $416,000 - $20,800 (down payment) = $395,200 Loan amount
- PMI
- $395,200 x 0.01 = $3,952/year
- $3,952 \div 12 = $329/month

In this second example I used the PMI rate of 1% to stay consistent with the first example. In all likelihood this rate would be higher if a homebuyer put a smaller down payment on a house.

A PMI payment of $329 a month is not significantly more than a PMI payment of $312 for putting an extra 5% down. But when we look at the cost of financing the extra $20,800, it adds up quickly.

The difference in a 20% down payment versus a 5% down payment on a house is about $740 a month more. Putting a larger down payment on a house will help homebuyers qualify for a more expensive house.

4

Chapter 4 - Interest Rates - The Forgotten Monster

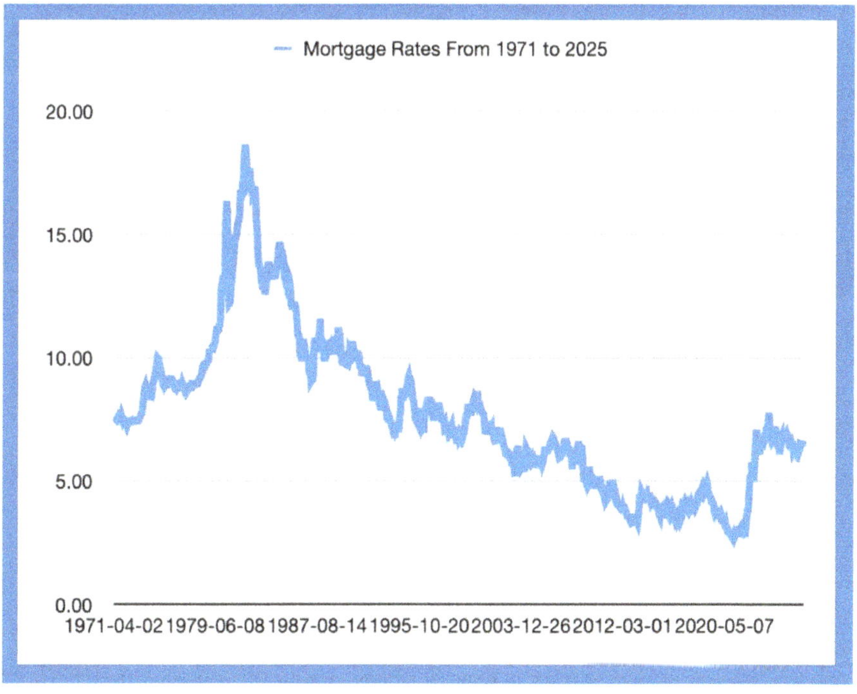

Federal Reserve Bank of St. Louis

Interest rates conveniently get left out of the affordability argument. Not because it is secret, it's more due to the fact that when included, it challenges the narrative that some want to perpetuate.

In 1975, the average 30-year fixed mortgage rate was 9%. By 1979 it reached a high of 11.2% and shortly after that in 1981 it reached 16.6%. These rates are unimaginable to Millennials who never lived through a time where interest rates were so astronomically high.

What exactly does it mean to have an interest rate of 16.6%? Remember that chart from chapter 2 when we explored principle and interest payments on 30 year fixed loans of $100,000 across different interest rates ranging from 3% all the way up to 16.6%? At 3% that payment was $422 and at 16.6% it was $1,394.

Over the life of these loans you would have to pay a total interest of $51,777 on the 3% rate loan and $401,840 on that 16.6% loan. This is not a small difference and that home with a 16.6% rate could easily be considered an asset trap.

How Rates Quietly Determine Affordability

When you hear stories of Boomers buying cheap houses you are more than likely hearing stories about those who bought before the mid-to-late 1970s. Those who bought between 1979 and 1983 with rates between 12% to 16% probably had different stories to tell.

Millennials today are faced with rates that are higher than the all time low rates of 2020 to 2021 but nowhere near as high as the early 1980s.

Debt-to-Income Ratio

Lenders use a metric called debt-to-income ratio to help determine if a prospective borrower will be able to afford a house. Traditionally, a debt-to-income ratio over 28% means that the borrower will not be able to afford the loan. There are exceptions to this rule and a lender will analyze each prospective borrower's total financial situation before approving a loan.

Let's look at an example of how debt-to-income ratios are used in conjunction with different interest rates:

Assuming a $280,000 Mortgage and $300/month for property taxes and insurance. Applying a 28% debt-to-income ratio.

- At a 3% mortgage rate, a borrower would need to make $63,471 a year to comfortably afford this loan.
- At a 16.6% mortgage rate, a borrower would need to make $180,257 a year to comfortably afford this loan.

To qualify for the same loan at such a high rate would require an income of almost 3x more. Interest rates and income both impact affordability in a big way.

Principal vs Interest: Where Does Your Money Go?

Another critical aspect of interest rates is how they affect the ability to build equity in a home. The higher the interest rate, the less equity is paid each month. This is easy to see on this chart below. At 3% a $100,000 loan will pay $172/month in principle (equity) while at 16.6% it will only pay $10/month in principle (equity). Understanding how interest rates affect your ability to build equity over time is an important consideration when buying a house.

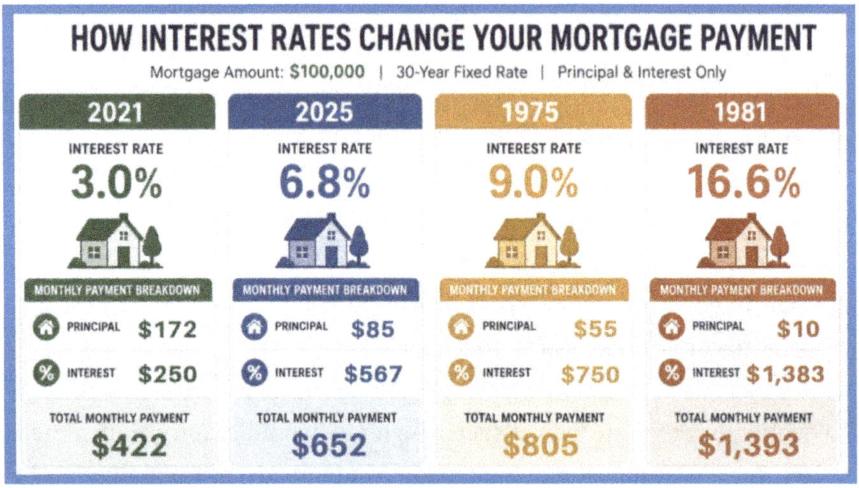

Why 2025 Is Hard But Not Historically the Worst

The housing market in 2025 is genuinely difficult. A household earning $83,730 faces a median home price of $416,000 with a 6.8% mortgage rate. This is a debt-to-income ratio of about 36% which exceeds the traditional 28% affordability threshold

While this debt-to-income ratio is a stretch, it was not the worst affordability environment in history. That time was in 1981. The debt-to-income ratio at that time using median income and median home prices was around 73% which was completely unaffordable. The only way anyone could remotely afford a house at that time was to either have an unusually high income or a very large down payment or both

5

Chapter 5: Income Then vs Now

Median Household Income from 1975 to 2025 Both in Nominal and Inflation-Adjusted

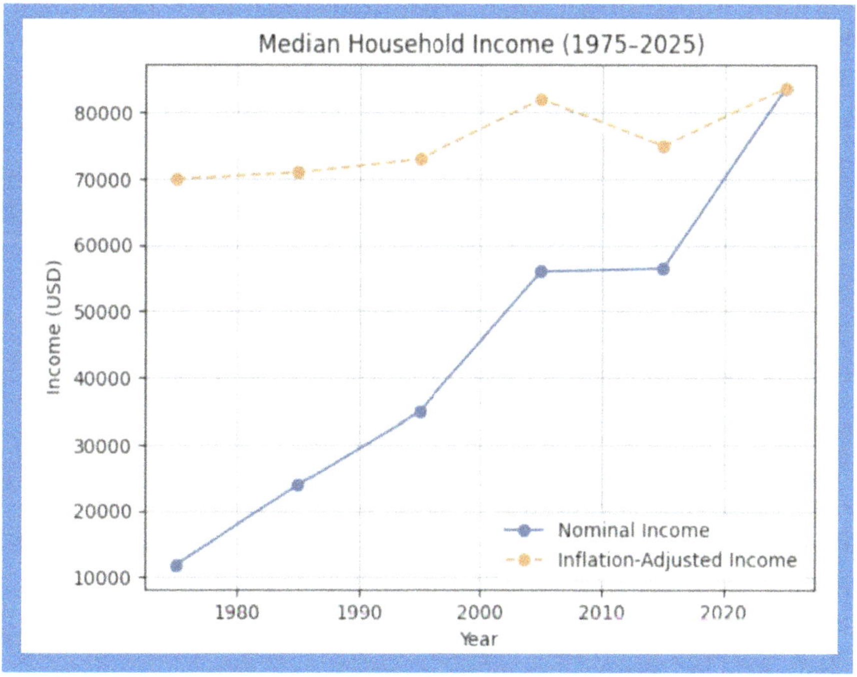

U.S. Census Bureau, U.S. Bureau of Labor & Statistics

The median household income in 1975 was $11,800 a year or about $983 a month in nominal terms. But adjusted for inflation, this would be about $71,000 in 2025. Comparing that to the median household income in 2025 of $83,730, there is no question that households made less money in the 1970s than they did in 2025, even when you adjust for inflation. The real challenge is understanding why. We are going to dive a little deeper into that in this chapter.

The Multiple-Income Shift

When we talk about household income between decades we have to understand there are important differences in what that measures. A couple important factors are things like; How many people make up that household? And how many people in that household are earning income?

In 1975 the percentage of households with two or more income earners was 43.1%. I have to admit this number surprised me and I had to check its accuracy from multiple data sources like the BLS and Census. I would have expected it to be much lower but this is indeed true.

Here is the breakdown of household income earners in 1975:

- 1 Income: 37.1% of total households
- 2 Incomes: 33.1% of total households
- 3 or More Incomes: 10.0% of households
- No Incomes: 19.8% of households (mostly from retired persons and students)

Only 37.1% of households had a sole income earner in 1975. If you scroll through social media nowadays you would think that number would be 90% or more. I can't tell you how many posts I read saying things like "in the Boomer's day they could buy a nice house with one income making minimum wage and raise a family of 4". Of course this was not true.

This is one of the many misconceptions from those who didn't live in that time.

In 2025 the percentage of households with more than one income earner was harder to find data for. The closest figure I could find was from the Tax Foundation which shows 41% to 46% of households with multiple income earners. Furthermore, if you break this down even more you will see that dual-income earners with children are even higher at 66%. A figure that isn't all too surprising as the costs to raise children are very high.

Here is the breakdown of household income earners in 2025:

- 1 Income: 32% to 35% of households
- 2 Incomes: 35% to 38% of households
- 3 or More Incomes: 6% to 8% of households
- No Incomes: 20% to 22% of households (mostly from retired persons and those on assistance)

The biggest surprise here is that single earning households dropped only a few percentage points from 37.1% in 1975 to between 32% and 35%.

The increase in multiple income households, while not as pronounced as I expected, has played a role in home ownership affordability. For many of these households the shift from a single-income earner to a multiple income earner household created a one-time purchasing power boost.

Adding a second income allowed households to afford a lifestyle that would not be possible without it. As more households became multiple-income households, more homebuyers' demand for nicer things began to rise. In simplest terms, when demand rises, so do prices. Those with multiple-incomes could afford these things and those without needed to add income earners to "keep up with the Jones". This created a reliance on multiple-income households that we still have today.

Why Household Structure Matters for affordability

In 1975, households had flexibility. Most of these households had only one income earner and if they did have a second income earner, that person generally only earned about 26% of the income that the main breadwinner made. If times got rough economically speaking, the non-income earner would go to work or increase their hours worked to ride out the rough patch.

In 2025, households lack flexibility. About half the households in the US have dual-income earners (49.1%). Unlike in the 1970s, 29% of dual-income earners make similar wages. This means for many, a second income isn't a luxury, it is a necessity. If one income is lost, this creates a financial crisis for that household.

Single-Earner vs Dual-Earner Incomes

First, let's look at what type of income we should use when analyzing housing affordability. Some have entered the housing affordability debate arguing that a single-earner income should be used. Others have argued that a true measure should be whether a minimum wage single-earners income should be used. The truest approach is to use median household income. This doesn't mean that household income from 1975 was a perfect reflection of household income from 2025, but it is the best measure we have to go with.

The biggest argument that those who wish to use single-earner income in our measurements is that most household income in 1975 was a single-income earner. While this is true, other aspects were at play. That single-income earner went to work while their partner stayed at home to raise kids and run the household. There was no need for daycare costs or maid services. Dining out was a rare occurrence because the stay-at-home partner would prepare meals.

These were all very different situations in 2025. Single-earner income households were extremely rare for married couples with children. About 66% of married households had dual-incomes. Because of this, part of that extra income had to be allocated towards daycare and other expenses.

The argument that minimum wage earners salaries should be used is just not a reasonable suggestion. It doesn't mean that this argument isn't being perpetuated on the internet. I have personally seen people make absurd claims that a single earning Boomer could earn a minimum wage salary and afford a house, raise a family and go on vacations regularly. Let's look at the minimum wage in 1975. It was $2.10 per hour.

$2.10 x 40 hrs week = $84/week x 52 weeks = $4,368/yr

That would mean a house would cost someone making a minimum wage in 1975, working a full-time job, 9 times their annual income. The debt-to-income ratio on a median house would be around 70%. Totally unaffordable!

Where You Earn Your Income Matters

Whenever examining the United States housing market we use national data. The problem with national data is that income varies greatly from one region to another. It's common to have two different experiences from people who earn similar incomes. Where these people live and work will be some of the largest factors on whether or not they will be able to afford a house.

It's no secret that workers in big metropolitan areas tend to earn a higher income than those in rural areas. The hardest part about this affordability debate isn't just compiling information about different time periods, it's also about finding a way to standardize a bunch of regional data into national data. The median household income in San Francisco, California was $141,000 a year in 2025 but in Dayton, Ohio it was only around $46,000 a year. This is a drastic difference and it makes comparing these two areas very difficult. We use national data for both income and house prices but those living in areas that are higher or lower than the median will have very different personal experiences.

In San Francisco the median house price in 2025 was around $1.5 million. The high median wages in that area does not make up for the high median house prices. This is more than 10 times that median household income and it means that buying a house in San Francisco is essentially unaffordable.

By contrast, In Dayton the median house price in 2025 was around

$240,000. This might seem like a very low price but when you factor in the median household income of only $46,000 a year, this means a house was slightly more than 5.21 times the median income in that area. The national average in 2025 is 4.97. While this is higher than the national average, it wasn't drastically higher.

Since we are using median house prices, let's look at some other areas where the median house price was at different price points compared to the national median. Here is what you would get for the median price of $416,000 in these areas:

- **Lancaster, Pennsylvania** - This price would get you an updated rancher or split-level home with 4 bedrooms, 2 bathrooms on a little more than a ½ acre of land.
- **Hollywood, Florida** - This price would get you a 2,000 square foot 3 bedroom, 2 bathroom home with an attached garage.
- **Atlanta, Georgia** - This price would get you a 3 bedroom, 2 bathroom home with an in ground pool.

Looking closer at each of these cities we will see how they compared to the national median income. In Lancaster county, PA the median household income was about $58,000 in 2025 and the median house price in that area was $346,000. This meant that even though the median house price in Lancaster was lower than the national average it would take about 5.97 times their median annual household income to purchase a house. This would consume more of their income than the national average of house purchasers.

For Hollywood, FL the median household income was around $67,000 a year. This was below the national median income of $83,000. The median house price in Hollywood sold for about $490,000. Because the median house price is higher than the median national house price and the median income is lower, this means to purchase a median house in this area will take about 5.90 times a household's annual income.

In Atlanta, GA the median household income in 2025 was around $86,000 a year. This is higher than the national median. The median house price in this area was $360,000. Because the median household income in this area is higher than the national median household income and the median house price is lower, this means it took less income to purchase a house. In fact, it only took 4.19 times a median household income to purchase a median house. This means compared to most of the United States, Atlanta was a better value for purchasing a median house.

6

Chapter 6: Size Matters

It is not a secret that the size of a median house has grown substantially over the years. In fact, it has grown by about 30% since 1975. The next question you might ask yourself is “does size really matter when it comes to price?” Let’s look at what truly matters when it comes to the size of a house and what has little to no effect.

In 1975, the median house size was 1,500 square feet. On average this was a ranch or bungalow-style house with 3 bedrooms, 1 bathroom and a garage. The rooms were small, closet space was minimal and you would consider yourself lucky if you were a child that didn’t have to share this space with a sibling.

By contrast in 2025, the median house size was 1,950 square feet. These houses were generally Colonial or Craftsman-Style homes with 3-4 bedrooms and an “Excess” (guest) bedroom, 2 ½ baths, larger closet and other storage spaces. These houses were more likely to have a master suite and each room was larger on average. You were unlikely required to share a room with a sibling as household sizes have declined throughout the years.

How Does Size Increase Costs?

Not all things that are bigger cost more. But when it comes to housing this is usually the case. It's a really simple concept on the surface. If it requires more material to make or build a product, it will cost more to make. This is true in real estate as it is in apparel.

Lumber - a larger home requires more lumber to frame than a smaller home.

Roofing- a larger home requires more shingles and other material. Not to mention a lot of modern designs have gone away from the standard A-frame roof to a more complex, multi-faceted design with intersecting planes. This not only adds material costs but also labor costs.

Electrical System - modern homes have 200-amp standard electrical throughout the house compared to 100-amp in many older homes. This means thicker gauge wiring and more of it to cover all the modern code requirements of an electrical outlet every 6 feet along walls.

HVAC - At a minimum, the HVAC unit for a larger house will have to be larger. Some homes require multiple HVAC units. Then add in all the duct work and you will quickly see how a larger house is more expensive.

There are many more added costs when building a larger house like plumbing, finishing, kitchen size and foundation size but I think you understand the point.

Size Does Not Increase All Costs?

While there are many things that cost more due to their size, some things cost the same or less. Take for instance the cost to acquire land. One of the biggest misconceptions about housing is that doubling the size of a house doubles the cost. It does not matter if I build a 1,500 square foot house or a 3,000 square foot house on that ½ acre plot of land. In reality, it rarely works that way.

Land Matters

Speaking about land costs for example. Let's say a builder buys a half-acre lot.

They need to determine what size home to build on it. Should it be:

- 1,500 square feet
- 2,300 square feet
- 3,000 square feet

The price they paid for the lot isn't changing much. If it fits on the lot according to zoning laws, the land costs will be the same. In expensive areas, this can be a huge deal. In some markets, literally half the price of a home is just the land itself.

Permits and Fees

Lots of permits and development costs are fixed or only somewhat dependent on square footage.

This includes:

- Permit applications
- Utility connection fees
- Survey costs
- Administrative costs

Developers often pay similar fees if they build a home that's a few hundred square feet bigger or smaller. Building permits on a quarter acre lot will likely cost nearly the same whether your home is 1,500 square feet or 2,500 square feet.

Labor Efficiencies

Labor can also increase at a decreasing rate. Let's say you want to build a shed.

A 200 square foot shed will probably require twice as many materials as a 100 square foot shed. It probably won't require twice as many workers. The workers are already there. The equipment doesn't need to be doubled. The crew has already prepared the job site.

Construction works the same way. If a home is 50% bigger, it won't necessarily cost 50% more to build because labor costs don't exactly scale. This is another reason builders prefer building larger homes. The extra square footage can allow them to earn more without proportionally increasing costs. As a result, they make more money.

Builders Aren't Building Smaller Homes

You may wonder why builders don't just build smaller houses if they are more affordable. Well, they just don't have the incentive to do so. Say a developer buys land and infrastructure to develop a subdivision. They need to build roads, connect to utilities, pay for permits, hire engineers, and purchase the land in the first place.

The cost of those items:

- Roads
- Utilities
- Permits
- Engineering
- Land

They need to be recouped by selling the houses. If a builder makes significantly more profit on a 2,500 square foot home than an 1,800 square foot home, there's a strong financial incentive to build much larger houses. Builders want to recover their investment. In most markets, that means building as large as they can, not as small as they can.

Builders Don't Make Homes Affordable Because They Don't Have To

It's why starter homes are so scarce. Unfortunately for buyers, builders aren't prioritizing affordability. They're maximizing their profits. Do new houses look more expensive because it's significantly bigger than older homes? Sure. But that doesn't mean home builders are solely responsible for America's affordability crisis.

Size Matters When Examining Housing Affordability

New homes simply have more square footage. That has made them more expensive. However, that isn't the only reason affordability has worsened since the late 20th century.

Other factors include:

- Supply constraints
- Population growth
- Increased cost of financing a home
- Increases in regulations

The reason housing affordability has been trending worse for decades is because of...I know this is going to sound bad...multiple reasons. Don't let that discourage you though. Understanding all the reasons why homes have gotten more expensive is the only way to reverse those trends.

Size vs. Affordable Homes: Comparing Apples to Apples

When we say new housing is less affordable than older housing we're not necessarily comparing apples to apples.

In 1975, a median home was significantly smaller than a median home in 2025. Here is what the average homeowner gets today that they didn't in the past. Wondering why your grandparents' home was so much cheaper than your new place?

Today's home buyers get:

- More square feet
- More comfort
- More privacy
- More tech
- More energy efficiency
- More amenities

That's not an exhaustive list but you get the point. More of a house equals more money.

The real question is whether those extra amenities are things you personally need. That's a question every buyer should ask themselves. Unfortunately, not every buyer will have the opportunity to answer that question. If home builders solely build large homes, buyers will only have large homes to choose from.

So merely demanding more affordability won't fix the problem if the market doesn't offer affordable options.

Summary

The average American house was about 30% larger in 2025 than it was in 1975. That increase in size has made homes less affordable.

But comparing the price of a new home to the price of an older home isn't fair. New homes simply offer more space and more amenities.

Comparing the price of a home in 1975 and a home in 2025 isn't comparing the same product. Don't forget that the next time someone complains about rising housing prices.

7

Chapter 7: Luxury Became Standard

One of the biggest differences between 1975 and 2025 is that consumers have become more demanding and will not settle for anything less than perfection. I saw this first-hand during my time in the real estate industry. The number of times I had a client come into the office with high expectations and a low bankroll was countless.

We did not get to where we are today overnight. All these comforts we have today in our homes were once aspirational to many in 1975. But in 2025 these expectations have become the minimum acceptable standard.

When features that added an extra $5,000 to $15,000 each to the cost of a home in 1975 became mandatory expectations in 2025, this proved to be a structural barrier to entry for most first-time homebuyers.

The 3 Types of Luxuries

There are 3 main types of luxuries we have in today's housing market that weren't common in 1975. All of them add to the cost of a house and make it harder for developers to build modest homes.

Here are the 3 main types of luxuries:

1. **Aspirational Luxury Creep:** These are luxuries that current buyers are demanding. The buyers do not need these features but they want

them.

2. **Building Code Luxury:** These are luxuries that have been mandated for legal or legislative reasons. The buyers do not have a choice but it still adds to the total cost.
3. **Product Improvement Luxury:** These are the features that may be technically optional but a buyer will not purchase a home without them.

Some examples of Aspirational Luxury Creep are stainless steel appliances, granite countertops, soft-close kitchen cabinets, 3 car garage, finished basement and French doors leading to a large backyard.

In 2025, living in this world where we open up our homes to everyone on social media, we want to put our best foot forward and these features have become standard. None of these features are necessary. If our stoves are white or black they will still cook food. We have substituted functionality for Aspirational luxury.

In 1975, many of these things seemed unattainable. People did not need to impress strangers online. Mostly because there was no "online." No Instagram stories, no Facebook posts and no searching for validation on the trending tab. The only people invited into their homes were family, friends and neighbors living in the same conditions they lived in.

Another part of Aspirational Luxury is when homebuyers demand to live only in the most trendy areas. As you can imagine, buying a home in these areas usually results in a premium price. In addition to these trendy areas, some homebuyers want to buy a house in the best school districts. Most people would understand this aspiration however it does come at a price.

Building Code Luxury isn't really a luxury anymore. In 1975 there were fewer building codes and few safety standards. In 2025, there are fire separations standards, standards related to buildings being able to withstand seismic activity, wind resistance and energy efficiency standards. While the energy efficiency standards will end up saving the homeowner money in the long-run, there is a large upfront cost. Even though I listed this as a luxury, a homebuyer doesn't have a choice to exclude these features.

These features are usually very expensive and they often require a great deal of time. As an example the average time to obtain a permit to build a home has increased from a few months to a few years. Carrying costs alone during this time has added extra costs to a new home that was built in 2025.

The last one we are going to talk about is what I call Product Improvement Luxury. These are things like Central Air Conditioning, double or triple-pane windows and more than one bathroom. Buyers have grown to expect these features in a house and they simply will not purchase a home without them. Of course all of these things are optional, including Central Air Conditioning (I grew up in a home my parents bought in 1985 with no AC).

While these improvements might be optional, many have grown accustomed to these products. Even though I grew up in a house with no air conditioner, I wouldn't buy a new house without it today.

How Does Luxury Increase Costs?

Let's examine some of these luxury costs and how they impact the price of a home in 2025. The largest luxury cost by far would be Central Air Conditioning. In the 1970s fewer than 30% of new homes nationwide were built with Central Air. Of course there were regions like the south where around 60% of those homes had it. The installation cost of Central Air Conditioning in 1975 was between $2,500 - $4,000. Inflation-adjusted that's around $14,000 in 2025 dollars. Since then the cost of installation has come down to about $5,000 - $8,000 in 2025.

I have included some of the luxuries homebuyers can choose from today in a list with an estimate of what those upgrades cost in 2025 dollars. For this list I chose the low-end for each of these improvements. In total, it added over $30,000 to the cost of a home. Not all these features are required upgrades:

WHAT HOME UPGRADES COST IN 2025

Plan Today for a Stronger Tomorrow

Features	2025 Estimated Cost
Stainless appliances	$2,500
Kitchen upgrades	$6,500
Bathroom upgrades	$8,000
Flooring upgrades	$2,000
Insulation	$8,000
Central AC	$5,000
Window upgrades	$6,000
Total Estimated Cost	$38,000

Upgrades Add Comfort. Maintenance Protects Value.

THE AMERICAN HOMEBUYER REPORT

Everyday Luxuries That Become Regular Expenses

One of the most difficult parts of comparing housing affordability across generations is understanding that the product itself has changed—not just the house, but the entire lifestyle that surrounds it.

When many people imagine middle-class life in 1975, they often picture something that looked remarkably similar to today. A nice house, a couple of cars, a television, and a comfortable lifestyle.

The reality was very different.

Many of the things we now consider necessities were either luxuries, rare conveniences, or simply didn't exist in 1975.

This does not mean that modern life is necessarily better or worse. It simply means that the cost of being "middle class" has changed dramatically.

Today's households often spend money on things that previous generations never had to budget for.

Some of these expenses are optional. Some are necessities in modern society. Most fall somewhere in between.

Multiple Vehicles

The typical American household in 1975 was less likely to own multiple expensive vehicles. That's twice the expense for transportation, insurance, maintenance and fuel.

One car payment is hard enough to manage but when you add two car payments it makes qualifying for a home loan much more difficult. Not to mention that cars in 2025 are much more technologically advanced. This adds to costs. These aren't the metal boxes on wheels that your parents or grandparents bought.

So why does this matter to our housing debate? It is another obstacle that must be overcome to be able to afford a house.

In 2025 many households have:

- Two vehicles
- Three vehicles
- Large SUVs
- Pickup trucks

This affects housing costs because it changes expectations.

Builders have to consider this when planning and building a house. They have to build larger garages to fit these vehicles, wider driveways, and larger overall lots.

Even our vehicles have made our homes larger and more expensive.

Entertainment Technology

In 1975, few households had more than one television, one telephone or more than one stereo system.

In 2025, households often have more than one television, multiple smartphones, a whole host of electronics such as tablets, computers, gaming systems and much more. Internet services and subscriptions could also fall into this category.

Some of these are clearly luxuries. Others have become necessities in modern life. In addition to the sheer number of these things, many of them are also accompanied by a monthly fee.

A family can function without the internet today about as easily as a family in 1975 could function without a telephone.

The modern household carries expenses that previous generations simply never had.

The Cost of Connectivity

What does a typical house in 2025 have in it and how much would those things cost on average?

Internet:
$80–$100 per month

Cell Phones:
$100–$250 per month

Streaming Services:
$50–$100 per month

Cloud Storage and Apps:
$10–$30 per month

This can easily reach $3,000 to $5,000 per year.

In 1975, most of these expenses did not exist. That does not mean younger generations are splurging. It means the cost of participating in modern society has changed.

Convenience Became Standard

Let's look at some of the things that have become standard in 2025:

Food delivery - When I was a kid in the early 1980s, Domino's Pizza expanded to my town and that was our first exposure to food delivery. Today, a pizza place would most likely go out of business if it didn't offer delivery services.

Now, hungry patrons can get just about any type of food delivered, not just pizza. Of course this comes at a price. Food delivery apps serve as a middle man collecting a fee that restaurants never had in the past.

Online shopping - The internet wasn't a thing for consumers in 1975. Online shopping didn't exist but this doesn't mean people didn't shop from home. The most common way people shopped at home during that time was mail-order. I personally would circle toys in the Sears catalog that I wanted for Christmas.

Unlike today, it took between 6 and 8 weeks to get the things you ordered. Because of the complexity, people didn't use it as regularly as they use Amazon today.

Ride share services - With the advent of apps like Uber and Lyft ride share services have grown in popularity. These services have become part of our daily lives in some cases. In 1975, taxis served the same purpose of these apps however, because of the ease of use, these services are used much more frequently than taxis were used in previous generations.

Subscription services - Subscriptions are nothing new but the amount of subscriptions have increased greatly. When I was young, it was common for people to have magazine subscriptions or gym subscriptions but today we have subscriptions for everything. Music, movies, sports, storage, news, software and many more.

House cleaning - While this luxury isn't as common as the rest I put on this list, it is definitely more common than it was in 1975. This is due to more households being dual-income households. There simply is not enough time in the day for all occupants to work and tend to a household. This is especially true for larger houses which have become more common today.

Meal kits - For similar reasons to why house cleaning services have become more common, meal kits have grown in popularity in recent years. Companies have capitalized on the need for households to save time by selling meal kits of prepared food. They only need to heat these meals up and serve. Sort of the modern-day TV dinner.

Many households today spend thousands of dollars annually on services that previous generations simply performed themselves. Time has become more valuable. Convenience has become a product. And convenience is expensive.

The Hedonic Treadmill

Economists sometimes refer to a concept called the hedonic treadmill.

The idea is simple:

A luxury becomes normal. Then it becomes expected. Then it becomes difficult to live without.

A lot of things followed this pattern. Think about things like: Air conditioning, dishwashers, and smartphones. They all followed this pattern.

Eventually, people stop viewing these things as luxuries entirely.This is why I think the housing affordability debate gets so heated between generations.

Older generations lived without these luxuries and when they bring these things up to newer generations, those people don't see these items as luxuries.

They become necessities in our minds. Yet their costs remain very real. And these costs can be the difference between homeownership and a lifetime of renting.

Does This Mean Boomers Had It Easier?

Not necessarily.

A household in 1975 gave up many conveniences most families today struggle to live without.

A household in 2025 will have conveniences our grandparents couldn't have imagined.

This isn't to say that one is better than the other. The point is when we only look at home prices, we ignore that the standards of what it means to be middle-class have shifted tremendously.

Today most families buy:

- More square footage
- More privacy
- More comfort
- More technology
- More convenience

Those things are not free.

8

Chapter 8: Hopelessness

If there is one obstacle that could prevent millions of young adults from reaching their financial goals, it's not high interest rates. It's not rising home prices or even student loan debt balances. It's hopelessness.

Home prices being more expensive than ever is a common social media topic. Everyday millions of people read headlines telling them homeownership is "dead", that the American dream is gone, or that Millennials or Generation Z will "never" be able to buy a house.

There is truth to all those statements. However, there is also a lot of hyperbole. Yes, home prices are high. Rent takes up more of the monthly income than it did for previous generations. Putting away money for a down payment can seem impossible.

The problem arises when thinking about how difficult it may be makes it seem impossible in our heads. Once you believe there is no hope, you are far less likely to take the small steps required to make an ambitious goal possible.

It shifts your thinking from:

"This is going to take time." to... "Why bother?"

That mindset is the death of long-term financial goals.

How Giving Up Creates Financial Failure

When someone believes homeownership or building wealth doesn't matter, small numbers like saving an extra $50-$100 per week doesn't seem like it will ever be enough to overcome high median prices.

When you think about it in the context of one month or even one year, they would be right. After all, that much money will not get you a house. Neither will two months' worth of savings. Many people don't even buy a house after saving for years.

Once you make the decision that small numbers "don't matter," you are far more likely to spend those small amounts on things that do feel like they matter. Like eating out, new tech gadgets, or shoes.

Why does that create a problem? A few reasons:

Someone who believes small numbers don't matter misses out on years of compound growth by never saving. By deciding that "it doesn't matter" will likely never see meaningful savings to begin with.

Even if someone started saving 3 or 4 years behind someone else, they would have lost years of compounding and allowed inflation to run against their savings.

Looking for a Miracle

When the traditional path to wealth feels out of reach, humans naturally become more creative in how they search for solutions. Some people figure out investing early and begin their financial journey on solid ground. Others turn to risky alternatives in hopes of getting rich quickly.

Over the last several years many younger investors have been introduced to financial markets through avenues that promise life-changing returns in a matter of months or years. Instead of saving money traditionally, some people decide to make speculative bets with their disposable income. Trading stocks, cryptocurrencies, sports betting, and meme stocks.

The promises you can become a millionaire by buying the "next Netflix" have attracted people to speculative bets on nearly anything. Some sites like

Kalshi or Polymarkets even allow people to bet on elections and if a newly hired ESPN sports anchor will say a certain word within their first week of work.

Investing vs Speculating

Investing your money into a diversified portfolio and holding for decades is one of the most predictable ways to create wealth over time. Speculating on hot stock tips whose prices are wildly influenced by market trends is gambling.

Sure. Some people have been luckier than others with cryptocurrencies or trading. Others have lost their entire savings after a few bad trades. The issue isn't that these alternatives never work. But the risk of losing everything is much higher than patient investing.

If someone feels they have to risk it all on one "big score" because they can't possibly save enough for 10-15 years, those high-risk bets start to feel reasonable. This kind of thinking can be catastrophic to your financial health.

The statistics and historical data strongly favor patience and long-term trends. Betting on the "next big thing" is incredibly risky.

Outrage Culture and Social Media

Past generations complained about the economy too. Everyone loves to blame things on their parents' generation, but do you know how many people their complaints reached? A dozen? Several hundred at most?

Now we live in a world where negative opinions that would have once been vented in the local bar can reach millions of people instantly. Articles that declare, "Millennials will never own houses," spread faster than truth.

Posts that feature exact words like "You'll never be able to..." are shared far beyond their original posts. They receive engagement in the tens of thousands because people like seeing their fears validated.

The problem isn't that people are pointing out real challenges. The issue is that these articles rarely focus on the full story.

Readers will overlook:

- Regional market variance.
- Different paths to homeownership.
- House hacking or roommates.
- The power of long-term investing.
- How small monthly contributions can add up over decades.

Hopelessness is far more viral than reality. Constantly reading these articles can shift your expectations. Instead of thinking, how can I get there?" you start to believe "why should I try?"

Our unwillingness to wait

Waiting is another thing society has gotten very good at removing. Movies don't take years to release. Packages are delivered in 2 days or less. We can get food delivered to our doors in under an hour. Information is at our fingertips instantly.

Instant gratification has become one of the defining traits of modern culture. Except when it comes to building wealth. Saving money still takes time. Compound interest still takes time. Down payments and waiting still matters.

Our modern society wants you to think you can have everything instantly but expects you to wait years to build wealth.

"The Grind" Was Never Easy

Look at how people used to buy houses, and you would think they graduated high school or college and instantly were able to buy homes shortly after. That's far from the truth.

Most first-time buyers put themselves in financially stable positions by living with roommates or sharing apartments for years. They worked extra hours, skipped vacations, saved religiously, and drove older junker cars that broke down.

For first-time homebuyers years ago, many saved for their down payment for years to buy their first home. Nothing about waiting has ever been fun. But that has been the case as long as people have been buying homes.

Just because it may be a tougher climb in your market doesn't mean the rules have changed. Having patience has been a requirement with every generation.

9

Chapter 9: The Hidden Cost of Regulation

In 1975 the cost of regulation was cheap. On average a developer could purchase land, get the proper permits and begin construction on a whole subdivision in just months. There were far fewer regulations, zoning requirements were fairly straightforward and environmental reviews and impact fees were not a thing or in some cases, very minimal charges.

But in 2025, the cost of regulation has skyrocketed. According to the National Association of Home Builders, regulation costs account for about 23% to 25% of the cost of a new single-family home. To put this in perspective, if that new home cost $400,000, then $100,000 would simply go to cover these regulatory costs.

These costs include not only the permit fees and the environmental impact studies, but also includes the carrying costs of this multi-year process.

Environmental Regulations

Over the last 50 years people have become more focused on environmental issues. The National Environmental Policy Act (NEPA) enacted in 1970 has pushed many state agencies to focus on the environment. Any development project that requires discretionary approval must undergo environmental review. For a small subdivision of 20 homes, this might cost $15,000 to $50,000 and take six to twelve months. For a larger development of 200 homes, environmental impact reports can cost $200,000 to $500,000 and take two to three years to complete.

These studies are designed to measure the impacts the new development will have on things like air and water quality, traffic, noise and greenhouse gas emissions.

There are no guarantees that the project will be approved. If the findings are determined to be bad for the area the whole project could be scrapped. This will cost the developer an enormous amount of money with no guarantees of seeing a return on their investment.

Impact Fees

Impact fees are charges against the developer to fund certain infrastructure improvements like: Roads, schools, water and sewer systems and other public services. The thought process behind this is that these improvements could be very costly to the current taxpayer. If the local jurisdictions can get these fees from the developers it will lessen the strain on the taxpayer.

While this might help lessen the taxpayer strain, it adds a cost of about $8,000 per single-family home built and in some places it can be extremely costly adding $80,000 per single-family home built.

Permitting Process

The permitting process in 1975 was relatively simple. It took on average 3 to 6 months. In 2025, the process could take 3 to 5 years.

This delay in the permit process adds risk to the developer. Over the course of 3 or 5 years lots of things can change. What if build material costs skyrocket? If consumer buying habits change? Interest rates rise? So many variables to consider and these developers will naturally incorporate those costs into the final product.

Other Regulatory Costs

There are so many regulatory costs in 2025 that either didn't exist in 1975 or were so minimal that it didn't affect the price of a home as dramatically as it does today. Things like Building code compliance and Energy code standards.

You might be asking yourself why don't we bring reform to these regulatory burdens to streamline the process and bring down the cost of constructing new homes. That's a great question but unfortunately this expensive, long drawn out process makes a lot of people money. These are the lawyers, politicians and activists who stand to lose millions if this process is changed..

Who Does Regulation Impact The Most?

There is no question that over the years we have made advancements in building methods and materials to make homes safer and more environmentally friendly. The real question is, did we overdo it?

Regulation accounts for almost a quarter of the total cost of a new home. Because of this high cost, developers have an incentive to build bigger houses where their margins are larger. This creates conditions that reduce supply of smaller, entry-level homes in the market.

Prior to doing the research for this book I wondered why developers weren't building starter homes anymore. There is a demand for them but after understanding the high regulatory costs to build, I finally understood.

Let's look at an example: If a developer wants to build 100 single family homes on a piece of land they bought for $3 million. The developer has a choice to either build 2,500 square foot homes that they could sell for $600,000 and make a profit of $100,000 per home or build 1,800 square foot homes that they could sell for $400,000 per home and make a profit of $20,000 per home.

Both of these profit numbers might look nice but when you take into account that the total profits were over a 3 to 5 year period and this developer had to risk a lot of capital for just 5% or 20% returns over that time period, it's not so glamorous.

The figure below show this example in detail:

A Developer Has A Choice. If a developer wants to build 100 single-family houses on a piece of land they bought for $3,000,000.

The largest reason that developers chose to build larger homes is because of the fixed costs of land. Each plot of land can be used to build a big or starter home. Regulatory costs makes the incentive for developers to build bigger homes helping to reduce the footprint of starter homes across the United States.

10

Chapter 10: More People, Same Land

The United States in 1975 had a population of about 216 million people, in 2025 that population had grown to 340 million people. This was an increase of 124 million people or a 57.4% increase. At the same time, the amount of land in the US has not changed. Technically the US did add the Northern Mariana Islands in 1986. Though this is officially a self-governing U.S. commonwealth and it didn't really add to land availability.

The population of the US is highly concentrated on the coasts. In fact 80% of the population lives east of the 98th Meridian.

The typical supply-demand principles are not at play when it comes to housing. At least not on a National scale. But in large metropolitan areas, supply-demand principles are at play.

America has plenty of land, just not where people want to live. Part of the reason there are large areas of land in the US uninhabited is because that land is not ideal for living. Large areas of mountains, deserts, and swampland make it not conducive to building.

Populations tend to concentrate around big cities. This was more important 60 years ago before the interstate highways system was largely underway and before technology made work from home possible. Even though access has been increased, many people still want to live within a short drive to a large city.

What 124 Million Extra People Means for Housing Demand

To find out how these extra 124 million people will affect the housing market, we must first understand household formation differences. In 1975, the average household size was 2.94 people. In 2025, that average has dropped to 2.51 people per household. This might seem like a small difference but it really adds to the number of houses needed in the US.

The total number of houses in the US increased from 80 million units in 1975 to 149 million units in 2025. This was a total of 65 million extra units built in that time period. Housing units increased 86% while the population only grew by 57%. During this time period, the ratio of housing units to population actually increased slightly.

Even though the housing unit to population ratio improved, prices still increased and affordability deteriorated. This is because those new units were not built in places where they were needed most, the big cities.

New home construction was mostly concentrated in markets where land was cheap, regulation was not burdensome and demand was constant. New homes were not built in areas of the highest demand mostly due to expensive land and regulatory restrictions.

Housing units grew by 86% across the US from 1975 but only 18 - 38% were concentrated in the most expensive areas.

More Homes, But Not Enough

One of the biggest overlooked factors in this Boomers vs Millennials great housing affordability debate is the change in household formation. The ratio of people per household changed from 2.92 to 2.51. What exactly does this data mean for house prices?

Household ratios are important because it explains how many housing units are needed to shelter our population. The total population in 2025 was 340 million people and because the average number of people per household is currently 2.51 this means we need a little more than 135 million housing units. The US has about 145 million units but at any given time 14 million of those units are not being occupied. This constrains the supply of current houses and increases prices.

If the US maintained its 1975 household formation ratio of 2.92 the US would only need 80 million housing units.

Why Did The Household Formation Ratio Change?

There are many reasons why the total number of people per household has changed in the last 50 years. The rise in one-person households has been especially significant. Millions of apartments, condos, starter homes, and senior living spaces are occupied by just one resident. That is not a failure of the housing system—it often reflects prosperity, longer life expectancy, and greater personal independence. Widows and widowers living longer, young professionals delaying marriage, divorced adults maintaining separate residences, and retirees aging in place all increase the need for separate housing units.

The divorce rate in 1975 was less than 5% compared to around 40% in 2025. This is an important factor in the housing debate because it increases the number of units needed and puts pricing pressure on the whole market.

This means the housing challenge is not simply "too many people chasing too few homes." It is also that modern life requires more homes per person than previous generations needed. Even if the home building had kept pace with raw population growth, it could still lag behind household formation. A nation can add millions of units and still feel under supplied if each unit houses fewer people than it once did.

In that sense, shrinking household size quietly became one of the most powerful forces pushing housing demand higher—without adding a single new person to the population.

The Roommate Generation, Then and Now

Another missing piece of the housing debate that has mostly been forgotten is the roommate equation. Many Boomers spent their early adult years in shared housing, in cramped living conditions while delaying gratification until they could save enough of a down payment for a house. The median age of a first time homebuyer in 1975 was 29. This was about 11 years after these Boomers had graduated high school. That's 11 years of splitting rent with multiple roommates, often in less than desirable neighborhoods and delaying purchases of material goods and experiences just to purchase a less than ideal first home.

Many Millennials believe that Boomers had an easy path to homeownership because of the low nominal median house price of $39,300 but the truth is something very different. Contrary to popular belief, this pathway in 1975 was not "get a job, buy a house." It was "get a job, share a space, save aggressively, then buy a modest house in a marginal location, build equity then trade up." It was very rare for a Boomer to buy a house shortly after completing school, but that has been the narrative of late.

The modern societal shift in valuing independence and status has replaced the old mindset of quietly-modest accommodations. In 2025, having your own apartment is seen as achieving success even if that apartment is small. At the same time, having a roommate is perceived as a sign that someone is struggling financially.

Every generation experiences challenges that prior generations did not have to deal with. Millennials are no different. They have experienced a great deal of challenges that Boomers didn't have to deal with until a later age.

Social media has changed the way people perceive success. It has also created enormous pressure on today's youth by amplifying perceptions of success with posts about exceptional achievements (most of which are unverifiable), while hiding the true struggles that are faced by most.

With social media, it is not enough to simply have a place of your own, you must have the nicest furniture with stylish home decor. Those IG photos need to impress your friends, even if these are friends you have never met in real life. While in 1975, that 29 year old who saved for 11 or 12 years before purchasing his or her first modest home, furnished their living rooms with second-hand items. That worn couch from their parents basement with cigarette burns and a miss-matched chair would not get millions of likes in today's social media world, but it was a common right of passage many Boomers had to endure while building equity as they slowly grew professionally in their careers.

11

Chapter 11: New Expenses Nobody Had Before

One of the most common narratives surrendering the housing debate focuses around Millennial excessive spending. Specifically, the types of spending that weren't even possible in 1975, mainly because these technologies hadn't been invented yet.

This criticism is not completely wrong. Millennials spend a large percentage of their discretionary income on cellphone plans, video streaming services, music streaming, delivery apps, fitness subscriptions and other digital services. In total, the average monthly spend on subscriptions is between $270-$485 a month ($3,240 - $5,820 year).

On the surface this might seem like the answer to the affordability problem, but some of these services only replaced older versions. Take for instance a cell phone plan. It is true that Boomers didn't have cellphone plans but they did have house phones. A monthly phone bill is not something new, both Boomers and Millennials had phone bills. The largest difference is the cost of the cell phone itself far exceeds any phone or equipment a house phone would cost.

Other parallel expenses are video streaming services and music streaming services. Boomers may not have had them but they did have equivalent services. Instead of video streaming services, Boomers had video rental stores (although most of them came about in the 1980s) and a small number of them had cable (about 14%). Music streaming wasn't a thing in 1975 but music was purchased in the form of records and cassettes (and maybe even an 8-track tape).

Regardless of the fact that there were equivalents to these expenses, all of them are discretionary. And yes, even the cellphone expense is considered discretionary. Which means by choosing to avoid these expenses would result in increased savings.

Is Avocado Toast to Blame?

There aren't many financial phrases that have generated as much controversy as "avocado toast."

With just these two words, people on either side of the housing debate know exactly what this implies. This is that Millennials simply spend too much on discretionary purchases. Of course the Millennials argue that no amount of skipping brunch can overcome soaring home prices, student debt, and rising living costs.

Like many arguments in this book, the truth lies somewhere in the middle.

Avocado Toast Doesn't Cause Sky-high Home Prices

Ok, so what is avocado toast then? Spoiler alert: It's not actually toast. Dropping $15 on brunch is not why median home prices ballooned to $416,000 in 2025. Skipping one breakfast isn't going to fund a down payment. However, choices do add up.

And while we are dismantling avocado toast myths, it's also not accurate to say how you spend your money doesn't matter. Purchasing a home has never been easy and it always requires sacrifice.

Your grandparents sacrificed in different ways than you. They bought smaller homes with fewer bedrooms. Often, not every child in the household even had their own bedroom. As a family they didn't take extravagant vacations. The cars they drove were often very basic. There were fewer "conveniences" and previous generations had to save years before buying a home.

A Millennial's sacrifices looked different in 2025, but they are no less real. What has changed since 1975 is a category of spending that economists call recurring conveniences. Instead of one large purchase, people are now making dozens of convenient purchases every month that barely seem like they're even happening.

Food delivery apps are a great example. The convenience is what you pay for.

Say someone orders delivery twice per week. Food delivery isn't always cheap. The average delivered restaurant order with menu markups, service fees, delivery fees and tips comes out to be about $35.42.

$70.84 spent per week on food delivery doesn't seem like a lot. For most people two food deliveries a week feels affordable. Maybe it even feels fancy. But rarely is wealth built quickly. It's usually earned over years of repeated small decisions.

What if you stopped making those small decisions with your dining budget?

What if you took the average $70.84 spent per week on delivery and invested that into a diversified stock market index fund?

We know from history that the U.S stock market has gone up roughly 10% on average per year over long periods of time. Remember this number because we'll be using it again.

Earlier I mentioned that the median first time homebuyer in the 1970s put away savings for approximately eleven years.

What if we took that same amount of time and invested our food delivery budget?

Here's what happens over 11 years:

- Weekly Contributions: $70.84
- Total contributed: $40,516.48
- Estimated Value: $77,200

That begins to add up to about 18.5% of a $416,000 median home in 2025. Two food deliveries don't seem so harmless when you consider what could be. This chapter isn't really about food delivery costs, it's about spending habits.

I could write an entire book about the meals you prepare at home. The point is that food delivery is convenient and most purchases like it come with a hidden opportunity cost. What else are you spending money on that you could be saving or investing?

Coffee purchases, subscription boxes, impulse buys at the grocery store, unnecessary smartphone upgrades. There's an endless list of recurring costs that we acclimate too fast. Stop and ask yourself if your daily Starbucks coffee is worth 18.5% of the home you want to buy.

No one habit, regardless of how expensive, is responsible for the housing affordability crisis. But when dozens of small habits are paired with a high cost of living, they compound into a larger wealth gap.

Avocado toast is expensive over time, not because of one meal. It's because you could order that meal thousands of times.

The Secret Ingredient: Time

Time is one aspect of this entire process that's practically free. Our society is built around instant gratification. Today we expect everything to happen NOW:

- Netflix movies stream immediately
- Groceries get delivered to our door within hours
- Uber drives magically appear with the tap of a screen

We live in a world where time has been optimized out of nearly every service except building wealth. Unfortunately, when it comes to money compounding interest rewards patience, not hustle.

The average homebuyer in 1975 probably didn't save for a couple months and suddenly went to buy a house. They saved for years, went without certain items, and steadily earned enough money for a down payment. That hasn't changed. What has changed is our willingness to wait.

Never Mind Avocado Toast, The Real Problem Is Hopelessness

If there's one enemy to saving money, it's feeling like your dreams of homeownership won't ever happen. We hear it from every direction that millennials can't buy a house. News companies, family members, Twitter... they're all telling you something you already know;

Home ownership is TOO expensive! There's no way!

When you hear this message repeatedly it's easy to accept it as truth. Eventually people who believe homeownership is out of reach stop budgeting, stop saving and give up entirely.

They start to believe things like:

- Why save if I'm never going to afford a home?
- What's the point in sacrificing now if it's hopeless anyway?

Letting go of hope is far more expensive than any down payment budget. Once you accept that something is impossible you lose the motivation to take the small steps required to make it possible.

Far too often I've talked to people who started saving only to give up after a few years. They didn't know what they were missing because they stopped too soon. The problem wasn't that they didn't have enough money.... It was that they lost hope of ever having enough.

Look at the Bigger Picture

The cost of living in much of this country is far higher than it was for past generations. But that doesn't mean you are powerless to change your situation. Understanding the economy doesn't change the fact that homes cost more today. But it can help you understand how your spending habits fit into the bigger picture.

Personal finance and macroeconomics are not mutually exclusive. A tough marketplace requires smart choices.

As it turns out, Avocado toast is not why Millennials can't buy their first homes. This doesn't mean that what they spend doesn't matter. It does.

Housing affordability is influenced by both structural economics and personal behavior. We cannot control mortgage rates, zoning regulations or decades of under building.

But we can control whether today's convenience is worth sacrificing tomorrow's opportunity. Financial independence has never been built on one perfect decision. It is built on thousands of small decisions made consistently over many years.

The good news is that those decisions are still available to every generation. The path may be steeper than it was for some buyers in the past. But it is not gone. And the first step is believing that your future is still worth saving for.

Is Saving a 20% Down Payment Realist Anymore?

For a young person or couple just starting out in life, choosing to forgo expenses that so many others find hard to give up could really add up. In the last section I mentioned how small changes in spending habits can make a big difference.

Now let's look at a couple examples of how this is possible. Whether a Millennial cuts some of their discretionary spending or all of it, the savings power is undeniable.

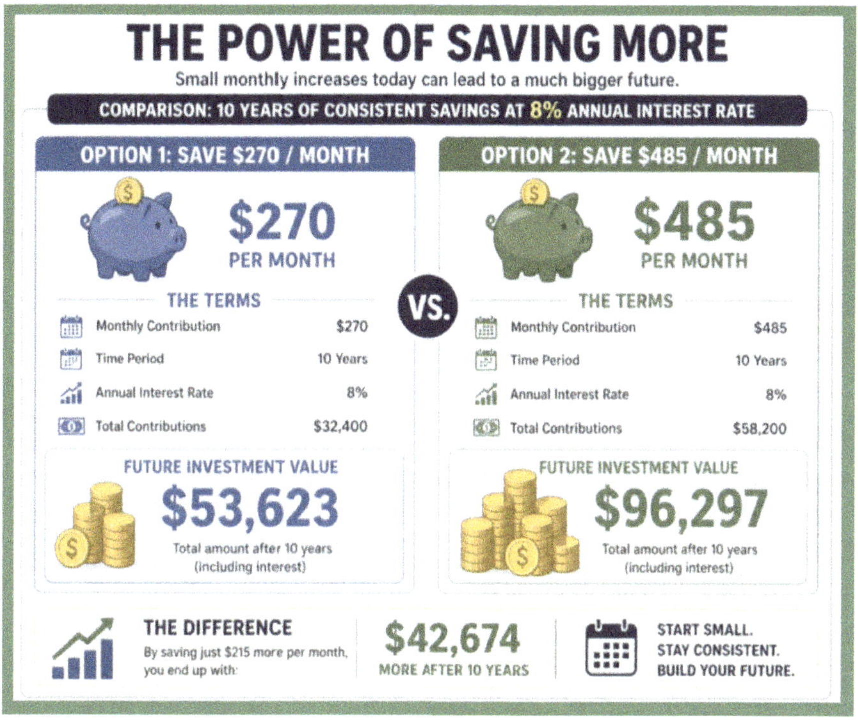

The previous chart is an example of how much money a Millennial could save in a 10 year period earning an 8% interest rate (10% is the average stock market rate of return), if they made either extreme sacrifices or modest sacrifices. The reason I choose 10 years is because Boomers saved for an average of 11 years before they were able to buy a house.

This could help solve one of the biggest narrative objections in the housing affordability debate. That is, how can a Millennial save enough to put a 20% down payment on a house?

An $83,200 down payment on a $416,000 median home might feel out of reach but it is possible with delayed gratification and frugal spending. A 20% down payment is the preferred down payment but there are other alternatives.

What To Do When A 20% Down Payment Is Not Possible

The difference between buying a house in 2025 and buying a house in 1975 is that financing has changed dramatically in that time. Some changes for the better, some changes not so much.

In 1975, assumable mortgages were commonly available. This was beneficial in the 1970s because a buyer was able to assume the loan and terms from the previous owner at the rates that owner paid. If the previous owner had a 6% interest rate and the current rates are 9%, the buyer could assume the 6% rate. While these were commonly available, not every seller wanted to assume the risk. If the buyer misses a payment it could affect the seller's credit.

Besides interest rate considerations, there were down payment considerations. While 20% is considered the standard down payment for a loan, there were options to put down less than this amount. The FHA allowed a 3% down payment on the first $25,000 of mortgages and 5% on any amount over $25,000 in 1975.

In 2025, assumable mortgages are largely unavailable but there are many programs that first-time homebuyers could use. It is not uncommon for first-time homebuyers to put less than a 20% down payment on a house. The median down payment of first-time homebuyers was 10%.

FHA loans allow as little as a 3.5% down payment. However, this does come with a catch. Any down payment of less than 20% usually is accompanied with a costly PMI (Private Mortgage Insurance) payment each month. This should be avoided whenever possible but sometimes it can be a way to purchase a house without waiting to save a large down payment.

Another loan option that is available for some first-time homebuyers is to take out a VA loan (Veterans Affairs). This is only available to qualifying people. Those who served in the military or eligible spouses.

VA Loans are some of the most beneficial loans to have for homebuyers. They don't require any down payment, PMI is not allowed to be charged and closing costs are limited. This means homebuyers who have VA loans could save hundreds of dollars a month and tens of thousands of dollars over the life of the loan.

Around 74% of first-time homebuyers who use VA loans put down no down payment. This is a lifetime benefit that can be used more than once and it helps those who have served obtain a home a little easier.

Over the years many things changed. There are more programs aimed at helping first-time homebuyers purchase their first homes. While the options might have been different in 1975 compared to 2025, in both cases there were options to reduce the down payment amounts.

First-Time Homebuyer Programs

Today there are more than 2,600 first-time homebuyers assistance programs across the US. Some of these programs are operated on the state level and what assistance they offer may vary.

These programs offer assistance in down payment help, closing cost reduction and interest free loans to help with some costs.

The exact assistance of a typical first-time homebuyer will vary but on average between $6,000 and $12,000. This might not be a total solution for coming up with a down payment but it is something that was not available to those in 1975.

I was interested to see exactly how much assistance a median first-time homebuyer in 2025 would qualify for. I used the down payment resource website to plug in the median numbers we are referring to in this book. The median home price of $416,000 and the median household income of $83,730 with only one occupant in the state of Maryland. The website said I "could" qualify for about 31 out of the more than 2,600 programs. Keep in mind that this was a very basic search and I didn't provide detailed information on our median example.

The search mentioned that it was possible to receive as much as $50,000 in assistance. While that would be terrific for a first-time homebuyer, it most likely is not common. Many of these programs offer more assistance to those with lower income and those with other qualifying factors like military service, native born individuals, rural homebuyers and those who are in law enforcement or teachers.

First-time homebuyer assistance isn't something new. While it wasn't as prevalent as it is today, it has been around for a while. In 2009, when I purchased my first home as a first-time homebuyer I qualified for the Federal First-Time Homebuyers Tax Credit which went into effect the same year.

This was an $8,000 tax credit. I had to wait until the following year to receive the credit when I filed my taxes. In my case, I didn't use it as a down payment or to assist with closing costs. I used it to remodel my kitchen. This tax credit was a big reason I chose the house I did. The kitchen was horribly outdated and hadn't been updated since the 1970s. But other than the kitchen, the house had good bones. Since I knew I would be getting this money, I lived with the outdated kitchen until the check cleared.

Just like for me, these programs can be incredibly beneficial to a first-time homebuyer. A large portion of these programs are for down payment assistance. About 74% of the over 2,600 programs focus on that. These programs offer a pathway to homeownership that wouldn't be available to as many without them.

If you are reading this book and are looking to purchase your first home, I suggest looking into these programs. Do your homework. It might just be the difference between qualifying for a home and not qualifying. Don't forget to look for assistance programs on the local level as well.

12

Chapter 12: Crippling College Debt

There is one expense that many Millennials faced that wasn't as common in 1975. That is the expense of college. Higher education costs have outgrown inflation in a big way. The combination of job requirements increasingly demanding a college degree for applicants and the availability of Government guaranteed loans helped increase demand for the pursuit of higher education.

Higher education hasn't always been a priority in the United States. In the early to mid-1900s the US was an industrial country with lots of manufacturing jobs. Most of these jobs didn't require a college degree and it wasn't seen as a necessary credential to advance one's career. Because of that, it was not common for high school graduates to pursue higher education. In 1975, only 14% of adults 25 or older had obtained at least a bachelor's degree.

In 2025, the number of adults 25 or older who had at least some college education has grown to 49.6%. This represents a significant difference in how education has become more common in the US. School systems have shifted from preparing high school students for the workforce to preparing them to enter college. This structural change came with a cost.

The Financial Cost of College

The cost of a college education has increased faster than inflation, this created a financial burden that compounds the housing affordability challenge. When comparing costs of college tuition from a public institution from 1975 to 2025, these costs rose outpacing inflation by a lot.

Cost for a four-year public university (tuition only):
1975 - $2,200 nominal ($13,240 in 2025 dollars)
2025 - $45,484 nominal

The difference in college costs from 1975 to 2025 is a significant factor in the housing affordability debate. Boomers had the ability to work part-time to save enough money to afford a college education. Even though the minimum wage in 1975 was only $2.10 an hour, it was enough for a college student to work 25 hours a week and pay for tuition from an average public university . Technically, this would be enough to pay for yearly tuition, room and board of around $2,275/year but realistically it would be a stretch. It would however be enough to cover the tuition alone (about $550/yr). Even in 1975 those students would most likely have to take out loans. Of course the loans would not be as large as Millennial's loans.This is a far different situation than what Millennials faced.

Even if a Millennial worked the same 25 hours a week as Boomers did, it would not be enough to pay for an average public university tuition, room and board ($29,000/yr) or even tuition alone ($11,371/yr) for that matter. Their Federal minimum wage was $7.25 an hour. Because of the Millennial's inability to pay for college in the same way a Boomer did, student loans became more prevalent.

This graphic shows the difference in struggles between Boomers and Millennials when it comes to paying for college while working part-time.

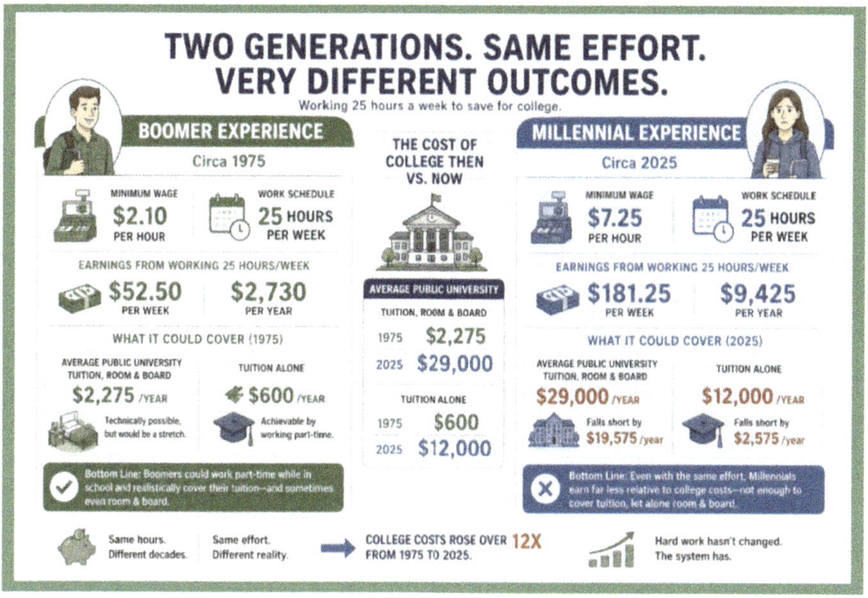

Beyond The Initial Cost of College

The initial cost of college is only a small piece of the total cost. The fact that many Millennials must take out student loans ensures this cost will be experienced far beyond graduation day. So how does this affect housing affordability? Those student loans must be paid back, usually over a period of 10 years after graduation. That is 10 years of added monthly expenses.

In 2025, the average monthly student loan payment was $400 a month. That $400 a month will reduce the ability for a potential homebuyer to qualify for a loan. Lenders use debt-to-income ratios to help determine if someone qualifies for a loan. If a borrower's monthly debt payments are over 43% of their gross monthly income, it would usually disqualify the borrower from getting a loan. Ideally, a borrower should keep their debt-to-income ratio under 28%.

The difference between a homebuyer with student loan debt and one without student loan debt can be significant. It can reduce the total amount a lender will lend to a borrower by tens of thousands of dollars.

So what is the potential impact of mortgage qualification?

Buyers earning the median yearly household income of $83,730 would equate to $6,978 a month with a $400 a month student loan payment and no other expenses has:

- Debt capacity: $6,978 x 0.43 = $3,001/month
- Student loan burden: $400/month
- Final Capacity for housing: $3,001 - $400 = $2,601/month

Based on the high end of 43% debt-to-income ratio this would mean a buyer could afford a $400,000 house with a 20% down payment of $80,000 at a 6.8% interest rate. This is how that monthly payment breaks down:

- Principal & Interest: $2,086.16
- Property tax: $367
- Homeowners Insurance: $150
- Total Monthly Payment: $2,603

To show the real difference in affordability with the high cost of student loan debt we need to run this same scenario without the burden of a student loan payment. Using the same income information from our first example here is the break down:

- Debt capacity: $6,978 x 0.43 = $3,001/month
- Student loan burden: None
- Final Capacity for housing: $3,001/month

Using the same 43% debt-to-income ratio this would mean a borrower could afford a $465,000 house with a 20% down payment of $93,000 at a 6.8% interest rate. This is how the monthly payment breaks down:

- Principal & Interest: $2,425.16
- Property tax: $426

- Homeowners Insurance: $150
- Total Monthly Payment: $3,001

There is a real difference in housing affordability between those with student loan debt and those without. Student loan payments can result in about a $65,000 difference in house affordability. Since we know the median house was $416,000 in 2025, we can determine that a household earning a median income could afford a median house if they did not have student loan debt.

Besides student loan payments, there are other disadvantages that someone who attended college faced in the housing affordability equation. One that is rarely talked about is the opportunity cost of attending college.

The Opportunity Cost of Attending College

Almost anyone can tell you that the lifetime earnings of those with a college degree is far greater than those without one. On average those with a college degree earn about $1.5 million more over a 40 year career than those without a degree. On the surface this seems as though those with a college degree have all the advantages but there are some disadvantages as well.

There are two main opportunity costs that those who attended college are faced with. One, is the delayed earnings of attending university for 4 years. This is not only the loss of income but also in contributing to retirement. The potential loss of future gains due to compounding retirement savings four extra years earlier.

The other opportunity cost goes hand and hand with the first opportunity cost. This cost relates to the time it takes to save for a down payment of a house. Because those who attend college generally start working at 22 instead of 18, those 4 extra years not only puts them behind by just 4 years but often more than that.

In 1975, the median age of a first-time homebuyer was 29. That means a generation that for the most part did not attend college spent 11 years after they completed high school saving for a down payment on a house.

In 2025, the median age of a first-time homebuyer is either 34 or 40 depending on what source the data is coming from. There has been a great deal of media coverage reporting the National Association of Realtors (NAR) survey data claiming that the median age of a first-time homebuyer is 40 years old. This contradicts almost every other data source. The Federal Reserve Bank of New York reports the median age at 34 and specifically notes that the NAR's data is skewed. Based on other data like the American Housing Survey from the Census Bureau that reports the age of 33 and Redfin reports the age of 35. Knowing this information it seems the NAR is an outlier and some have questioned their methods which use surveys that can be biased. Other data sources use Consumer Credit reports and MLS data. Based on what I have learned, it's most likely more accurate to use a median age of 35 for this data. This excludes the NAR outlier stating the age is 40 and the Mortgage Bankers Association outlier that reports an age of around 32.

If we use 35 as the median age for a first-time homebuyer in 2025 and we assume this homebuyer attended college and graduated at 22, This will mean it would take them 13 years to save for a down payment after graduating. This is 2 years more than those from 1975 who did not go to college.

In addition to the extra 2 years it takes to save for a house, those in 2025 also miss out on the appreciation of a house they could've bought earlier. This is why so many Millennials feel as though they have missed out on the upside in the housing market that so many generations before them have benefited from.

Probably the largest opportunity cost that many Millennials have missed out on is the 4 years of compounded retirement savings. Let's take a look at two examples. They both assume monthly contributions to a retirement account of $400. One is for a term of 47 years which represents an 18 year old who entered the workforce right out of high school and the other a 22 year old who entered the workforce after college contributing for only 43 years. They both have a target retirement age of 65. The annual rate of return is 8%:

18 Year Old:

- **47 years @ $400/month**
- **Total Contributions: $225,600**
- **Ending Balance: $2,026,923**

22 Year Old:

- **43 years @ $400/month**
- **Total Contributions: $206,400**
- **Ending Balance: $1,432,799**

This means someone who entered the workforce right after high school will have $600,000 more for retirement than those who chose to go to college. The 8% rate of return is a very conservative rate as the market has averaged more than a 10% rate of return since 1928.

Because those with college degrees have higher lifetime earnings, they could in theory contribute more each month towards their retirement savings. But of course, they would probably have 10 years of paying the average of $400 a month to pay off their student debt. So even though they will make more money, they would most likely delay contributions resulting in lost compounding.

Compounding interest is often not fully understood. One of Albert Einstein's most famous quotes addresses this:

"Compound interest is the eighth wonder of the world. He who understands it, earns it; he who doesn't, pays it." — Albert Einstein

This is something I learned early in life. Growing up in the savings and loans era of the 1980s, I was able to put my grass-cutting money in a savings account earning a 5% interest rate. It really sparked my interest in savings when I took my passbook into the bank and learned that I had more money in my account than I actually deposited.

I was lucky enough to learn about compound interest at an early age.

Hopefully more people will get to experience the joys of what Albert Einstein called the "Eighth Wonder of the World."

Besides all of these opportunity costs mentioned already, there is another often overlooked one. Those four extra years of not working results in less job experience gained. Some jobs value experience over education and this will put some college graduates behind non-college graduates for promotions and advancement opportunities. This can have severe negative effects on the long-term financial situations of many millennials.

Crippled by student loan debt and the realization that some of their co-workers who choose not to attend college are advancing in their careers faster than they are, it creates a disdain for those who have more than them.

This does not mean that everyone who attended college regrets it or is disadvantaged. Some career paths value a college education over a lack of one. But even when those careers pay an above average wage, it takes time for the extra wages to equal the benefits of working right away. This is why I personally choose to attend college while working full time.

13

Chapter 13: What Still Works Today

After reading the last twelve chapters seeing just how complex the housing affordability issues are, you might be asking yourself what we can do about it. Some of these actions are societal changes that require large portions of the population to participate in enacting. Others are more personal choices which requires a shift in mindset and expectations.

Societal Changes

Societal changes are the most difficult to affect. This requires large groups of people to make certain changes that will bring down certain costs but might not be so easy to achieve. Thinking back to chapter nine when I talked about regulation costs, these are costs that have creeped up over the years. They have up-front costs as well as time costs. These have affected the median house price.

Getting rid of just a few of these regulatory costs sometimes requires an act of Congress. Seriously, an act of Congress! However, some of them can be addressed on a more local level. Regardless, it will take the ability to convince a lot of people that the current regulations are more burdensome than the benefits of them.

Some of those people you need to convince are not so easy to get on your side. Think about environmental regulations. There are whole government agencies with many employees who rely on these regulations for their livelihoods. There are Organizations who profit from the existence of these agencies, groups of people who have genuine environmental concerns and politicians who campaign on these regulations. Convincing all these groups would be no easy task.

Safety is another regulation that has added costs over the years but almost nobody is willing to sacrifice these regulations to help the affordability of a house. These are things like lead base paint restrictions, fire separations on row and town homes, seismic standards and wind resists requirements.

These societal issues are almost impossible to change once they have been initially enacted. There is a good chance that in the next 50 years there will be more regulations than we currently have today. While it is important to understand how these costs affect housing affordability, in reality it will be next to impossible to change. Maybe we should focus on the things we do have more control to change.

Changes in Expectations

Some of the changes we have more personal control of and an actual ability to change is our own expectations. In chapter seven I talked about how luxury has become standard. There is no greater example of this than in the housing market. Expectations have creeped so high that builders who used to specialize in low-cost basis housing have either adapted to these expectations or went out of business.

This is because the market has changed. In 1975, home buyers were happy with a 3 bedroom 1 bath house with a small kitchen and basic amenities. If a builder were to build that same house in 2025, nobody would buy it or the builder would have to reduce the price to a point that makes it unprofitable to sell. Even in preexisting houses people's expectations have creeped up.

My own experiences working in real estate has allowed me the opportunity to observe this over the years. It was not uncommon for prospective homebuyers to enter my office with lets say ”very stretched expectations.” Often they would tell me the location they wish to live in and their required size and number of rooms. When I found out how much of a home they actually qualify for, the conversations got difficult. I would show my clients what houses they could afford and they would claim that they "required" a 4 bedroom house. When I showed them 3 bedroom options in their budget they insisted the 4th room was needed. Most of the time this was more of a "want" than a "need."

They also "wanted" a big back yard and granite counter tops among other things. The point is, I saw first-hand how people's expectations have changed and those changes have added to the total cost of a house. When homebuyers understand that having realistic expectations will open a world of possibilities and could save them thousands, that's when things will begin to change.

House Hacking

Next on the list of things that might help with the housing affordability problem is house hacking. This is a strategy that some use to afford a house that might be traditionally unaffordable for that person's financial situation. This option may not be for all first-time homebuyers as it does add risk and work to the homebuyer.

House hacking works by combining traditional homeownership with a real estate rental model. This is how it's done: The first-time homebuyer would purchase a 2,3, or 4 unit house sometimes called a duplex, triplex or four-plex. They would live in one of those units and rent out the others.

The reason this works is because lenders allow the homebuyer to count the monthly rental income as additional income. This helps the homebuyer with their debt-to-income ratio. I explained debt-to-income ratios in great detail in the last chapter. Because of the improved debt-to-income ratio, homebuyers can afford a more expensive house. A homebuyer using house hacking gets into a larger home and starts building equity sooner. As that equity builds, they can later move to another home and continue to collect rent or sell out completely and upgrade to a larger home.

There are downsides to using this strategy. Rental management is hard work. Dealing with late payment, maintenance issues and the risk of vacancies could add a great deal of stress to a first-time homebuyer. Like I said, this is not for everybody!

Geographic Relocation

One major advantage Millennials have today that Boomers didn't have is that ability to work from home. Due to technological advances that were made over the last 50 years and the shift from a manufacturing country to a service based country, workers have options that never existed before. A worker can work from their living room coach in some situations.

Because of this, a worker can often live in a low-cost area but work in a high-cost area. This allows that worker to be paid a wage that is competitive in a high-cost environment but saves thousands by living in a low-cost neighborhood. Imagine working in San Francisco making $140,000 a year but having the ability to purchase a house and live in Ohio where the median house might be $280,000. This is a far cry from a median house of around $700,000 in San Francisco.

I understand that this will not work for all remote workers. Some jobs have rules about where workers live and some require remote workers to come into the office from time-to-time. But if this works for you, it might be an option to explore.

Smaller Starter Homes

If you have the ability to buy a smaller home it could help you save thousands. Nobody wants less of anything, but small sacrifices can really add up. In chapter six I discussed the differences in size between 1975 and 2025 and the challenges regulations have presented for home builders to build smaller houses. As a result, homebuyers in 2025 have a median size home that is 30% larger. This creates challenges to first-time homebuyers who would be willing to settle for a smaller house.

For the most part, new homes are being built larger but there are many preexisting smaller homes available on the market. A great way for

Millennials to get their feet in the door of homeownership at a reasonable price is to buy one of these smaller homes. It is especially hard to find a smaller home that hasn't been upgraded to today's standards. Finding one of these homes can build equity quickly if you are the type of person who doesn't mind putting a little sweat equity into it.

Increasing Income & Cutting Expenses

The obvious answer when it comes to housing affordability is usually not the easiest to implement. Everyone knows that if you increase your income, affordability becomes much easier and cutting expenses has the same effect.

There are many ways Millennials can grow their income. Technology has made "Gig Work" easier to get and do. This offers a pathway to increasing income that wasn't possible to Boomers. If a Boomer wished to increase income they had to apply in-person for a part-time job with defined hours. Today's gig work offers flexibility along with extra-income.

Many common gig work opportunities are things like food delivery apps and shared ride services. These can be turned on and off based on the availability of the worker. Boomers usually had a specific time commitment they were required to work in order to make that extra income.

Another way to increase income is to obtain more qualifications. This can be done today much easier than in the past. Online universities and training options are common now. Education was available during the Boomer era as well. That education was also less expensive but scheduling options and availability was not always feasible. Boomers couldn't take online courses because they didn't exist.

These extra qualifications can result in higher incomes and new career paths. Even in today's world this is not an over-the-night solution.

Let's look at some of the ways to cut expenses. In my opinion there is no better way to cut expenses than to choose to attend college part-time while working full-time. This isn't for everyone but it is a great way to save money.

Working full-time while attending college helps pay for college so that student loans can be avoided. There are sacrifices that must be made. The increased work-load of a full-time job and attending college means free time will be at a minimum. Giving up the traditional college experience is something so many people don't want to miss out on.

The amount of money saved is not just the tuition but the average of $400 a month for the next 10 years those loans could amount to. Many employers have tuition reimbursement programs where they pay some or all of an employee's college expenses. This benefit wouldn't be possible by attending college in a traditional manner.

Here is my own personal experience with part-time college:

- Started working full-time one week after graduating high school
- Built real world work experience and job qualifications
- 6 months into my employment I gained a CDL (commercial drivers license) qualification which resulted in more money.
- I attended college part-time at my local community college.
- My employer reimbursed my college expenses up to $2,000/year
- I spread out my Associate Degree education over many years to take advantage of the total reimbursement
- Transferred a state university while still working full-time and benefiting from tuition reimbursement.
- I also received a transfer scholarship which helped cover some of the costs of a state university.
- After my Bachelor Degree, I attended graduate school also while working full-time.
- Graduated without any college debt

The point of me sharing this path is to show the possibilities of graduating without college debt. It was not easy! I did have to pay some money out of my pocket even with tuition reimbursement from my employer but it was minimal. Let's look at some of the pro's and con's of part-time college:

Pro's

- **No Student loan debt**
- **Start building work experience**
- **Obtain qualifications**
- **Start retirement savings earlier**

Con's

- **Long hours working & studying**
- **Lack of college life (traditional)**
- **Lack of personal time**

Just like any other trade-off, the choice between full-time or part-time college comes down to your willingness to make these trade offs. For me, I was willing.

Besides college, there are many other savings that could really add up when focusing on expenses. Subscriptions are number one on this list. Mainly because most people forget to cancel their subscriptions after they stop using the services from them. Things like gym memberships, apps and magazine subscriptions are common road bumps. Canceling these memberships will most likely not solve the affordability problem by themselves but it's a good place to start.

14

Chapter 14: Corporate Home Ownership: Boogeyman or Saint?

You see it everywhere, newspapers, social media posts and even on the nightly news, "Wall Street is buying up all the houses!," "Corporations are destroying the American dream!" and so on. This narrative is filled with emotion but is it true? We will look closely at the actual data in this chapter to help us determine what effects corporate homeownership has on the market.

In certain areas of the United States, corporate homeownership of single-family homes represents 15% to 25% of house sales. This is not an insignificant number of houses. In these areas, homebuyers are facing many challenging circumstances. First-time homebuyers have found this environment especially challenging.

The Actual Numbers

The number of single-family homes owned by large corporations on a national average is relatively small (2% to 3%). Even though corporations represent such a small portion of the single-family housing market this doesn't mean that it doesn't affect the market. There are different types of corporate homeownership that exist. There are companies that specialized in different fragments of the housing market. Here are some of the companies and what segments they specialize in:

- **Single-family Rental Companies:**
- Invitation Homes, American Homes 4 Rent and Tricon Residential are some of the big companies in this market.

These are companies that specialize in renting single-family homes and each of them have thousands of rental properties under management. They are also all REIT's (Real Estate Investment Trusts) which are given specialized tax advantages provided that they meet certain requirements.

United States Current Housing Units

As of 2025 there were about 148 million housing units in the United States. Out of those units, 82 million were single-family homes. This is who owned those 82 million units:

- **Owner-Occupied:** 58 million homes (about 71% of the total single-family home market)
- **Individual Investor-Owned (1 to 9 properties owned by a landlord):** 18 million homes (22% of the single-family home market)
- **Institutionally Owned (10+ properties):** 2.5 million homes (3% of the market)
- **Vacant or Other:** 3.5 million homes (4% of the market)

Looking at the actual numbers it tells a story about the housing market. This might be a totally different story than you have heard on social media apps or in news reports. Institutions do not own enough housing units to affect price on a national basis. They do however own a large enough percentage of homes in a few specific areas of the country. Some of the areas where institutions own a large percentage of homes are:

- **Atlanta, Georgia:** 25% Institutionally owned
- **Jacksonville, Florida:** 21% Institutionally owned
- **Phoenix, Arizona:** 14% Institutionally owned

After learning about these areas with such high institutionally owned single-family homes you might assume that these are also the areas with the highest year-over-year price increases, but you would be wrong. From 2024 to 2025, none of these areas made the top 10 list of the highest year-over-year price increases. This contradicts the argument that "Wall Street" or "Large Institutions" are driving up home prices in America.

While the data is clear that these institutions are not driving prices up, they are negatively affecting first-time homebuyers in these highly concentrated areas. First-time homebuyers have a hard time competing with the "All Cash Offers" these institutions can make and the ability to buy multiple houses at one time without the need for typical contingencies like home inspections.

Those who argue for institutions buying single-family houses say these institutions are providing an important service. Their position is that these institutions have large amounts of money to spend on renovating houses. Houses that would not be renovated without this influx of money and sit vacant. A lot of these homes are turned into rentals which helps satisfy the demand for housing in these growing areas. Institutions buying these houses quickly is a good thing for existing homeowners too. Having too many houses on the market would drive down prices. This would negatively affect all current homeowners. Their existing homes would go down in value and limit any equity they may be looking to extract through refinancing or sales.

The other side of that argument is that if these houses were not purchased by institutions there would be more supply in the market pushing prices down. Some homebuyers in these areas would be willing to purchase a fixer-upper but competing with institutions makes this process more challenging.

15

Chapter 15: Real Estate Is Regional

Why Comparing Home Prices Across America Is Harder Than It Looks

The United States is not one housing market. It's thousands of housing markets each with their own unique qualities.

While national median home prices allow us to easily compare trends from year to year, they can sometimes be misleading. By calculating the average cost of homes across America, the national median obscures massive regional variations.

Someone buying a house in rural Kansas is not experiencing the same housing market as buyers in suburban Washington, D.C., Miami, or San Francisco.

Think of the median home price as the national thermostat. It can tell you whether America is hot or cold, but it cannot tell you about the temperature outside your front door. If we want to understand what's happening to affordability, we must look closer to home.

America Has Always Been Made Up of Local Markets. One of housing's unique characteristics is that it can't be moved. You can drive a car from Michigan to Texas. You can fly a television from China to anywhere in the U.S. But you can't pick up a house and move it to another city.

Because housing stock is fixed to a particular place, local factors matter more than they do in many other sectors of the economy:

- Job growth
- Population growth
- Availability of land
- Zoning laws
- Property taxes
- School districts
- Climate
- Transportation infrastructure
- Crime
- Amenities

...and more!

The dynamics between these factors can vary greatly from region to region. And because of this, it's possible for the national median home price to rise while hundreds of local markets remain affordable.

Market #1: San Francisco, California

On the expensive end of the spectrum, we have San Francisco.

San Francisco has seen years of strong job growth thanks to the technology industry, venture capital, and high-income workers moving into the area. But there was only so much land to develop. The city is surrounded by water. And for much of its history, zoning laws made it difficult to build new housing.

Home prices have soared as a result.

Even an average home by San Francisco standards can cost well over $1 million. And for many would-be buyers in the city, the challenge isn't getting a mortgage. It's saving up enough for a down payment.

Six-figure incomes are not uncommon in this market. And yet a software engineer earning $180,000 per year would still struggle to buy a home.

National headlines often come from stories about buyers living in expensive coastal cities. But those markets are not the whole story.

Market #2: Columbus, Ohio

About as far away from San Francisco's housing market as you can get in the continental U.S. is Columbus, Ohio.

Population growth has led to demand for more housing, but the city isn't restricted by the ocean on three sides. Developers haven't run out of land. When more houses are needed, builders have generally been able to push further outward.

Prices have increased as a result. But they're still a far cry from places like San Francisco, Los Angeles, or New York.

Households earning the median income for Columbus may still find housing unaffordable, particularly considering recent interest rate increases. But owning a home is substantially more attainable than in many other parts of the country.

Areas like Columbus are often what economists think of as "run-of-the-mill" American housing markets. Prices are important. Interest rates are important. Incomes are important too. But there are generally more homes available if demand continues to rise.

Market #3: Rural Kansas

Finally, consider a small town in rural Kansas.

Job growth and population may be stagnant. Demand for new housing hasn't skyrocketed. And there is plenty of room to build new houses if it does.

In some markets, you can buy a home for what would just barely be considered a down payment in major metropolitan areas. You could buy a three-bedroom house for less than the cost of a new Tesla.

That doesn't mean everyone who lives in rural Kansas is wealthy. In fact, lower home prices are often caused by lower wages, less employment opportunity, stagnant population growth, and weaker economic development.

Remember how demand is lower in this market? That's one reason housing is so affordable. Low home prices aren't the only measure of a region's prosperity. When discussing housing affordability, we should always evaluate prices in relation to income.

THE MEDIAN PRICE PROBLEM

Let's say we have three different markets:

- San Francisco median price: $1,400,000
- Columbus median price: $325,000
- Rural Kansas median price: $180,000

Simple. Easy to understand. But if we averaged these three prices together, what would the result tell us about the experience of buyers in these markets?

Not much.

There is a reason news agencies cover stories from San Francisco and not rural Kansas. One reason US News focuses on markets like New York and Los Angeles. National statistics only matter because they affect every city equally. But the cities themselves are nothing alike.

That doesn't mean the national median home price isn't useful. As a broad benchmark to measure affordability against year over year, it serves its purpose. It's just that the number can't possibly capture all of the factors that matter to homebuyers:

- Regional variation
- Migration
- Local wages
- Housing quality
- Property size
- Neighborhood desirability

...and more!

Sure, you can buy a house at the median price in San Francisco. And you can buy a median priced home in Columbus, Ohio. But those two homes will likely not be the same size, quality, or located in neighborhoods with the same opportunities.

LOCAL AFFORDABILITY MATTERS

National median home prices are important, but they don't tell the whole story. The United States doesn't have a housing market. We have thousands of local markets that vary widely by economy, population, regulations, and geography. Just because home prices may have gone up nationally doesn't mean they went up where you lived.

Americans' experiences buying homes can be just as different as the markets they live in.

16

Chapter 16: The Missing Million Homes

What Happened After 2008?

When discussing housing affordability, one question inevitably comes up:

If the housing market crashed so badly in 2008, why are homes so expensive today?

The United States experienced the worst housing collapse since the Great Depression. Millions of homes entered foreclosure. Home prices fell sharply in many markets. Entire subdivisions sat unfinished. Construction companies went bankrupt. Builders abandoned projects.

If housing became so overbuilt that it crashed the economy, shouldn't we still have plenty of homes today?

The answer isn't so simple. The housing shortage was not created overnight. It took more than fifteen years to build.

The Great Housing Boom

To understand what happened, we first need to understand the years leading up to the crash. Between the late 1990s and 2007, the United States experienced one of the largest housing booms in history. As a Realtor in the early 2000s, I personally had a front row seat to this housing boom.

Several factors fueled this boom:

- Low interest rates
- Easy mortgage credit
- Speculation
- Rapid population growth
- Expanding suburbs
- Rising home prices

Even though mortgage rates started the 1990s around 10%, it dropped to a low under 6% by 2003. To understand how significant this was you would have to realize that rates had never been this low before 2003.

The excitement of falling rates encourages homebuyers to buy. Houses were selling for more than their list prices sometimes. I remember helping homebuyers try to navigate this changing market.

It wasn't easy. Many of them couldn't understand why they needed to offer more than the list price of a home. After they were out bid a few times, they quickly learned. This helped home prices rise at a rapid pace.

I remember answering a flood of phone calls every time the Federal Reserve lowered interest rates. Even though the Federal Reserve's short-term rates don't immediately affect mortgage rates, that didn't stop the inquiries. Every news report mentioning lower interest rates resulted in more homebuyers looking to buy a house. Because interest rates helped fuel the housing market, more homes were needed to satisfy demand.

In addition to low interest rates, the availability of credit can only be described as a free-for-all. Just about anyone who wanted a loan could get one.

The rise of "NINJA" loans helped people get loans that they should never have qualified for. NINJA stands for "No Income, No Job, No Assets." Borrowers could qualify for a mortgage strictly based on their credit scores. Lenders didn't look into whether or not the borrower would be able to pay back the loan and didn't take into consideration all the obligations they currently had.

Another loan that compounded the issue even more was subprime mortgages heading into 2008. Leading up to the housing crisis of 2008, lenders were giving subprime mortgage loans to anyone that wanted one. Subprime mortgage loans are loans made to those who typically have low credit scores or no credit history. These loans had extremely high up-front costs. Meaning that the lender didn't really care if you defaulted on your loan because they were selling them to investors as fast as they could. So, lenders were approving these loans left and right knowing a high percentage would default. This wasn't a problem until they all defaulted at once leading to the 2008 housing crash.

Builders acted in almost every way that you would expect them to when housing demand began to ramp up. They built as many houses as they could. Neighborhoods were being built overnight. Farmers were selling their fields to be developed. Construction crews were working overtime. Housing starts reached an all-time high.

Everyone believed that housing would continue this upward trend forever. It didn't quite happen that way.

The Housing Crash Of 2008

The housing bubble of 2007-2008 when it popped left turmoil in its wake. Home prices plummeted. Mortgage defaults spiked. Foreclosures skyrocketed. Banks lost billions. Developers were stuck with land they couldn't sell. Projects were canceled. Builders went out of business. Some construction companies vanished.

The ripple effect of the popping bubble was more than just a housing recession. Confidence vanished. For years lenders, builders, investors, and consumers were all in survival mode. Rather than ramping construction back up too fast, we went too far in the other direction. For years we didn't build near enough houses to keep up with demand.

Housing Starts Plunged to Historic Lows

Housing starts is one of the best ways to visualize this. If you were building millions of homes per year before the recession but only built 700 thousand housing units per year after the recession, that is going to have a major impact.

Years after the recession hit, we were building new homes at a rate not seen since the 1940's. And we had far more people in America than our parents did back then.

This didn't dip for a couple of years. It dipped for over a decade. The population was still growing. Household formation was still happening. New families were still being created. They just suddenly weren't given new homes to live in. We stopped building houses.

Thousands Of Builders Went Out of Business

I know what you are thinking. Sure, we weren't building as many houses, but once demand picked back up builders just started building again. What you aren't accounting for is that thousands of builders went out of business over this time. And they didn't just open back up.

Small and medium sized builders were hit the hardest. Many of these smaller builders had been building homes for decades. They built relationships with contractors and subcontractors. They trained workforce on how to construct homes efficiently. When these builders left the industry, they weren't just sitting around waiting for things to pick back up. They retired. They moved on to different industries. They lost their businesses.

The entire construction industry lost years of building capacity. And that takes time to recover from.

We Lost Skilled Labor

Not only did we lose construction companies, but we also lost skilled labor. During the housing recession tens of thousands of construction workers left the residential construction industry.

- These folks included:
- Framers
- Electricians
- Plumbers
- Roofers
- Drywall Installers
- Concrete workers
- HVAC Technicians

And many more.

Where did they all go? Some left the industry. Some retired. Others became commercial construction workers.

Think about when housing demand started picking back up. Builders had projects, but they didn't have workers to complete them. We are still feeling the effects of this today. Labor is one of the biggest constraints on housing production.

You can't just build a subdivision because you want to. It takes thousands of hours of skilled labor to do so. And you can't instantly create thousands of skilled laborers.

Missing One Year Adds Up to Millions

While we do blame the housing crash of 2008 for millions of missing homes, it wasn't because we stopped constructing homes for just one year. The issue was we constructed less homes for multiple years.

Let's pretend that a community needs to build 100 new homes every year in order to keep up with demand. But instead of building 100 they only build

80. Now there is a shortage of 20 homes. The next year they built 80 again. Now we are up to 40 homes short of where we should have been.

40 million may not sound like a lot compared to our current shortage. But do this for 10 years. Add those missed houses up. That is essentially what we did on a national level.

Year after year we didn't build enough homes to keep up with demand. Researchers calculate this number differently. Some say we are 2 million homes short. Others say we are 5 million homes short. Regardless of where you fall, the shortage is massive.

And it wasn't because we weren't building any homes. It's because we weren't building enough homes to keep up with this growing population.

The population wasn't stopping growing just because we built fewer houses.

Nothing Stopped; Not Even Household Formation

We typically focus on the number of homes being built. But we often forget about population growth. Millions of new people have been added to the United States since 2008. They all need a place to live.

Whether it be:

- An apartment
- A starter home
- A rental property
- A single-family home

Millions of new households have been created through natural population growth alone. But household formation didn't stop happening either.

- People still married
- People still divorced
- People aged into new homes

People continued doing everything they always have that contributes to household formation. The demand was still there. But for many years we weren't building enough houses to satisfy that demand.

Why Home Prices Shot Up So Quickly

Buyers eventually returned to the market. And around 2019 when mortgage rates started to go down, they came back in full force. The issue was we didn't have enough homes to meet this sudden demand. Simple supply and demand. When there is too much demand and not enough supply, prices go up.

Remember this doesn't just apply to housing. If there was a sudden increase in demand for tennis shoes and the supply remained the same, the price of tennis shoes would go up as well.

The only difference is that the supply of tennis shoes could be ramped back up relatively quickly. Housing requires land, labor, and materials. Building millions of new homes takes time. Time that we didn't have because we were also dealing with:

- Labor shortages
- More regulations
- Higher material costs
- Land constraints
- Financing issues

You can begin to see why we are still feeling the effects of that housing shortage we created from 2008-2020.

Understanding the Housing Shortage Matters When Discussing Millennials vs Boomers

A lot of discussions around generational differences with housing focus on personal spending habits. Some people blame Millennials for spending too much. Others blame Boomers for getting lucky.

Both of those things might be true to an extent. But there is a lot more to this story.

One of the reasons millennials appear to be struggling more to buy a home than past generations is because they are literally competing with every other person who wants a home. And there are millions of people that we aren't building enough houses for.

Anyone that wants to buy a home in 2025 is not fighting for housing against the 1970s. They are fighting against:

- The housing boom
- The housing crash
- Builder bankruptcies
- Labor shortages
- Years of under building
- Increased population
- Increases in household formation

Lots of factors went into the housing market that millennials and Gen Z are experiencing today. And none of those factors favored the millennial looking to buy a home.

Was the Housing Shortage Preventable?

Sure. But there's a reason thousands of builders went out of business. When the housing market crashed in 2008, no one was calling for more construction. People were worried about too much construction. Everyone from builders, to lenders, to regulators, to investors became a lot more cautious.

In retrospect people were likely too cautious. But had everyone rushed back into construction as soon as the recession hit lows, we would have had a different problem on our hands.

The Moral of the Story

When someone asks you who to blame for rising housing costs, the knee jerk reaction is to lash out at the easiest target. Maybe millennials are spending too much. Maybe boomers are staying in their house too long.

But some of the reasons why housing is so expensive today is because we don't have enough of it. Between 2008 and 2020 we didn't build enough homes to keep up with demand. As a result, we are paying the price today.

17

Chapter 17: Every Generation Thinks the Last Had it Easier

Selective memory is one of the most powerful forces in human psychology, and it plays a role in this housing affordability debate. The boomer who bought a home in 1975 does not remember the anxiety about whether rates would rise further. The fear of layoff in an era before the modern safety net. The commute on an interstate that was, in 1975, still under construction in many sections. The neighborhood that has since gentrified spectacularly but which, in 1975, your parents thought was a bad idea.

In 2025, everyone who was from that 1975 era seems to remember paying $40,000 for a house but they seem to have forgotten all those uncomfortable details.

These stories help fuel a fantasy that buying a house was easy for Boomers. Millennials hear stories from their grandparents about buying their homes at a low nominal price and their houses are now worth half a million dollars or more. It's a very compelling story but it's a matter of perspective. While their grandparents might have been able to purchase a home before or after the mortgage rate spike in the late 1970s or early 1980s, others weren't so lucky.

What goes unmentioned are the countless number of people who lost their homes when interest rates spiked or had to sell their homes for a loss when rates topped out at 16.6% in 1981.

While some of the neighborhoods Boomers bought houses in improved a great deal over the years, some did not. Those who were unsuccessful tend not to share their stories of despair at the holiday dinner table. They go quietly unnoticed by a generation who can't seem to imagine a $40,000 house being forced into foreclosure.

Three Rust Belt Cities That Prove Home ownership Doesn't Always Lead to Immense Wealth Accumulation

CLEVELAND, DETROIT, AND PITTSBURGH: When buying a home did NOT lead to becoming a millionaire

One narrative you often hear about housing in America is how easy it was for Boomers to buy a house and become wealthy. They simply woke up one day and decided to buy a home.

This narrative is largely derived from looking at markets like San Francisco, Seattle, Boston, or Washington, D.C. and seeing how home prices have appreciated exponentially higher than inflation over the last five decades.

However, that isn't the case everywhere.

In fact, there are some of the largest metros in America that paint a completely different picture.

If you want to understand how misleading national headlines can be when it comes to housing, let's look at three metropolitan areas that have experienced population decline, de-industrialization, and sluggish economic growth:

- **Cleveland, OH**
- **Detroit, MI**
- **Pittsburgh, PA**

These metropolitan areas were some of America's largest industrial cities. Through the mid-1900s, they were the shining stars of America's manufacturing economy. They provided highly compensated union jobs, comfortable middle-class living, and relatively inexpensive paths to homeownership.

However, as time went on these areas missed out on much of the dramatic appreciation we've seen in other housing markets.

In 1975 these weren't cheap cities to live in. Far from it. The U.S. economy was very much built on manufacturing, and these metros had some of the higher incomes in the country as a result.

Median metro home prices in 1975 were roughly:

Cleveland $40,000
Detroit $38,000
Pittsburgh $36,000
United States $39,300

They were virtually neck and neck with the rest of the country.

Purchasing a home in Cleveland, OH or Detroit, MI was not buying in a significantly below-market place. Homebuyers were buying into thriving metropolitan areas that were considered the heart of America.

I wouldn't have thought it either if you asked me back then which cities would go on to under perform America by a wide margin over the next 50 years.

How They Compare Today

Fast forward to 2025. The national median existing home price is approximately **$416,000.**

Now compare that with these metropolitan areas:

Metro Area	Median Home Price (2025)
Cleveland	$241,000
Detroit	$352,000
Pittsburgh	$255,000
United States	$416,000

All three cities are now significantly below the national median. Pittsburgh and Cleveland are among the most affordable large metropolitan areas in the country, while Detroit remains far below many major metropolitan markets despite a recent resurgence.

It was so bad in Detroit that it had to file for Chapter 9 Bankruptcy. After 13 years, Detroit's bankruptcy case just closed in the first half of 2026.

So why did these cities struggle when so many other cities were prosperous?

.

During the second half of the twentieth century, the United States transitioned from a manufacturing-based economy to one increasingly driven by:

- Technology
- Finance
- Healthcare
- Professional services
- Information industries

Many of the highest-paying manufacturing jobs that once powered Cleveland, Detroit, and Pittsburgh disappeared or declined significantly. Then population growth slowed. In some areas, populations declined. Demand for housing came to a screeching halt.

And unlike coastal markets, these cities generally had ample room to build additional housing when demand increased.

The result was simple:

Home prices appreciated much more slowly than the national average.

The Inflation Test

This is where the story becomes particularly interesting.

If we adjust the 1975 national median home price of approximately $39,300 for inflation, it equates to roughly $236,505.

Now look again at these metropolitan areas:

Cleveland and Pittsburgh are remarkably close to the inflation-adjusted national price of a typical house from 1975.

In other words, a homeowner who purchased a median-priced home in these markets fifty years ago may have barely outpaced inflation after accounting for maintenance, property taxes, insurance, and transaction costs.

But what it doesn't account for is size. The median square footage of a house in all of these areas went up. They didn't go up as high as the national median size. Most only went up a few hundred square feet. This is most likely one of the factors in why home prices in these areas remain among the most affordable in the nation.

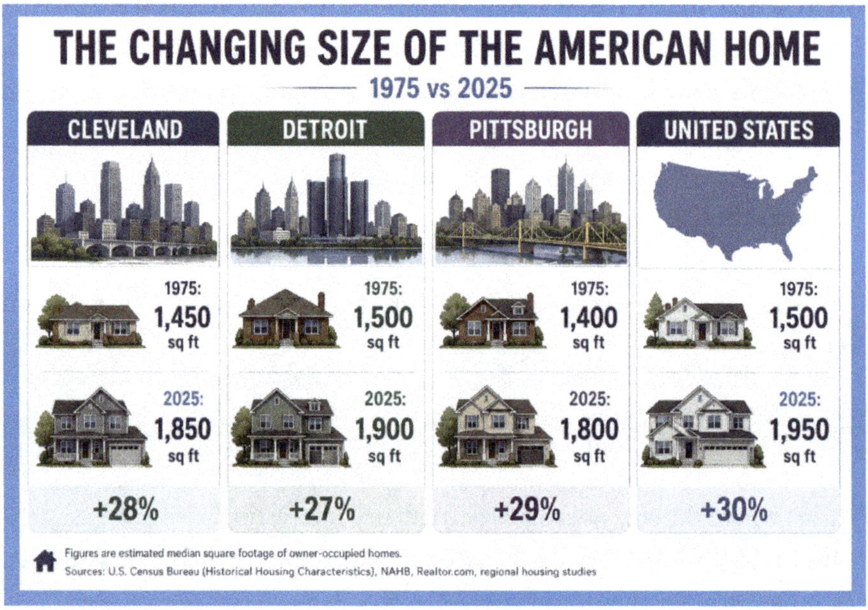

While the median house size across all of the US went up 30%, the median home size in these three markets only went up an average of 28%. Its lower but not significantly lower.

As I mentioned many times before in this book, house size alone is not the only reason prices are where they are today but it does play a significant role. The overall economics of an area is probably one of the most significant factors. The old adage of Location, Location, Location holds true.

That is a very different experience than what occurred in places like:

- San Francisco
- Seattle
- Boston
- Los Angeles
- Washington, D.C.

In those markets, homeowners often accumulated enormous amounts of housing wealth simply because of where they happened to buy.

The Neighborhood Effect

Zooming down to the neighborhood level, the story gets even more extreme.

Take your pick:

- Cleveland
- Detroit
- Pittsburgh

Home values in many neighborhoods across these cities today are equal to or even less than their inflation adjusted values from 50 or 60 years ago.

This is what happened in many neighborhoods that:

- Lost population
- Lost industry
- Saw their schools crumble
- Saw crime escalate
- Are stuck with older housing stock
- Have not seen any meaningful investment in new housing

For the homeowner in these areas, their housing was a way to have a roof over their head. It was not a wealth creation engine. Home ownership is not wealth creation by itself.

Location! Location! Location!

Buying a cheap house did not make the Boomers rich. Buying the right cheap house did.

Someone who bought a middle-of-the-line house in suburban San Jose in 1975 could have experienced vastly different results than someone who bought a similar house in Cleveland. Both could have made great investments based on their stage of life. One could have created millions of dollars of home equity. The other could have simply kept up with inflation.

The Myth of Broad Housing Wealth Across Generations

"When boomers bought houses, they were really cheap!"

When people say things like this, they're unknowingly only looking at the survivors. The truth is much different than this narrative implies.

Countless Boomers who lived in Rust Belt cities did not see meteoric appreciation. They didn't become housing millionaires. Their houses kept pace with inflation or only experienced modest gains. Many neighborhoods have seen essentially zero real appreciation over the past 50 years.

Focusing on the people with housing wealth is survivor ship bias. We listened to the San Francisco homeowner and the Boston homeowner and the Seattle homeowner because their outcomes were extraordinary.

What we don't listen to enough are the stories of the suburban Cleveland homeowner who has only kept up with inflation for 50 years.

How Social Media Amplifies Resentment

The housing affordability debate has become more prevalent and more toxic online. Outrage is rewarded by the algorithms on these platforms. The most popular online posts are those that cherry pick old house listings showing new houses for sale in 1975 for low nominal prices. What they don't show is the square footage, lack of air conditioning, and amenities today's homebuyers would not even consider making an offer on.

The comment sections of those posts are just as short-sides as the posts themselves. Hundreds or even thousands of comments are quick to confirm that homebuyers have it especially hard today. They fail to consider the five variables we discuss in this book or even two of them for that matter. The old saying is that "misery loves company" and these social media posts tend to have plenty of company.

It doesn't take much scrolling in that comment section to find someone angry with Boomers because they themselves can't buy a house. "The Boomers created a system that worked for them while it disadvantaged future generations" This isn't an exact quote because I would like to keep this book clean. It certainly captures an example of the anger seen on social media about the housing affordability debate.

If these posts and comments were accurate, it would talk about the five variables that tell the story of why current house prices do not reflect past prices. Comparisons would be done on an apples-to-apples basis and the "influencer" and/or keyboard warriors would offer suggestions to help make housing more affordable. Of course none of that will ever happen because those things wouldn't help push these posts on those social media platforms. Those algorithms reward discourse.

Needs Versus Wants

Over the past few decades we have seen a huge shift in what people think are necessities. This shift in thinking has detrimental effects on affordability. As more luxuries become standard and more people expect to have them, costs skyrocket.

We have seen these expectations formulate in all areas but especially in the area of purchasing homes. The number of homebuyers who will not sacrifice their wants to settle for their needs have increased. There is nothing wrong with satisfying and seeking wants, the problem is when the wants become too expensive to reasonably satisfy.

Examples of this include prospective homebuyers demanding that a house needs to have more bedrooms than they realistically need. Other common wants that homebuyers seek are things like extra bathrooms, larger closet space, big backyard, remodeled kitchens and many more "none essential" wants.

Homebuyers in 2025 could help reduce their overall costs in purchasing a house if they were willing to only focus on their needs.

Throughout this book I have mentioned the median home price over-and-over again but what most people don't take into account is that it is rare for a first-time homebuyer to buy a house at or above the median price. This median home price is for "all" homes purchased. The median price of first-time homebuyers specifically in 2025 was around $355,000 to $380,000 according to Realtor.com. I was not able to find a reliable estimate of the median first-time homebuyer price in 1975 but it would most likely be less than the overall median. Oftentimes, first-time homebuyers need to make sacrifices that other homebuyers may not need to make.

Understanding how sacrificing some wants to satisfy needs will not solve the affordability issue alone. It takes a collection of many variables mentioned throughout this book.

18

Chapter 18: The Houses Didn't Disappear

The Myth of the Vanishing 1975 House

One of the most common arguments in the housing affordability debate centers around the availability of the same homes from 1975. A lot of young homebuyers seem to think all those houses just disappeared.

"Those homes no longer exist" say many Millennials.

Most of them are comparing the median 1,500-square-foot home from 1975 and a 1,950-square-foot house loaded with amenities from 2025. There is some truth in that statement. The average home built in 2025 was much larger than the average new construction home built in 1975.

Buyers today expect central air conditioning, multiple bathrooms, larger kitchens, walk-in closets, and attached garages.

Those 1975 houses did not disappear. They are still here, and there are millions of them across the country.

Existing Housing Stock Matters

When people compare the median new home in 1975 to the median new home in 2025, they are comparing two different products. Most Americans do not buy newly constructed homes. So looking simply at newly constructed homes alone will not produce the most accurate data.

The United States has tens of millions of houses built before 1980. A large number of these homes remain close to their original size. A 1,500-square-foot ranch house built in 1975 still exists in a number of neighborhoods across the US.

A buyer searching in Ohio, Pennsylvania, Michigan, or many other markets can find homes that closely resemble the typical home purchased by a Boomer family fifty years ago. As you might imagine, this adds fuel to the housing affordability argument. Millennials point out that the prices of these homes rose even though the size of them remained the same. Inflation and size cannot account for the price increase.

The Inflation Test

Let's say your house sold for the 1975 median price of $39,300. After accounting for inflation that home would cost you about $236,505 today.

Now let's say you want to sell your home. You look at what sold recently in your neighborhood and think you should get $236,505 for your house because that is what your old house would cost today. However, homes that are just like your 1975 home sell for much more than $236,505. So, what gives?

There is more to housing values than inflation. That is why I am trying to take every possible aspect into account when valuing a house from one period against another.

Here are some of the reasons your house is worth more than the inflation adjusted value:

- Land values go up.
- Neighborhoods age.
- Fewer occupants per household.
- Jobs become more accessible.
- The population increases.

- And many of these homes just changed over time.

Let's focus on the last point. When we look at a house that was built in 1975 and is still standing in 2025 it has had fifty years of changes.

Roofs have been replaced. Windows have been upgraded to double pane or triple pane windows. Bathrooms have been renovated. Kitchens, HVAC, electrical and floors have been updated along with many other home improvements.

By the time you buy a home built in 1975, you aren't really buying a 1975 house.

Sure, you may have the same footprint and same square footage. You may even have some of the same cabinets and fixtures. But the roof is likely new.

Sure, you can try to find a house built in 1975 that has not been touched. But for every house like that, you can find another that has had $50,000 of improvements.

Comparing Apples-to-Apples

When we pay full price for that upgraded 1,500-square- foot ranch built in 1975, are we paying for the original house? Or are we paying for all the improvements that have been added through the years?

Pretty much both. It is the investments homebuyers make that nobody accounts for.

When we talk about housing prices we normally only discuss the purchase price. We don't talk about what was done to the house after it was purchased. Consider two houses built in 1975 right next door to each other.

House #1

Zero updates for 50 years.

House #2

- New kitchen
- Two-bathroom remodels
- New windows
- New roof
- New HVAC system
- New electrical service
- New flooring
- New outside improvements

Fast forward to 2025.

House #2 likely absorbed $100,000 of renovations. Maybe more. But when that home sells for $400,000 EVERYTHING is considered part of the sales price. The purchase price from 1975 and 50 years of capital improvements.

Buyers start comparing a mid-updated house to a 100% original house built in 1975. That is not an apples-to-apples comparison.

Even though "house #1" received no updates over the past 50 years, it probably benefited from improvements of other comparable houses in the area.

When appraisers value a house's value, it heavily weighs what other "like" homes have recently sold for in those areas. The appraiser will take into account the lack of improvements but this is not an exact science.

Appraisers might be aware of specific improvements on a few houses that sold in the area but rarely are aware of all of them. So when they are looking at comps (comparable houses), they really don't know all the information that resulted in that house selling for what it sold for. This house "house #1" ends up getting appraised for and ultimately sold for more than just the inflation adjusted price over time. It benefited from grouping that house with others.

How Many Inflation-Priced Houses Exist?

Using the inflation-adjusted equivalent of the 1975 median home price ($236,505), there are still a substantial number of homes available throughout the United States.

However, they are not distributed evenly. Most are concentrated in lower-cost regions of the Midwest and South. Meanwhile, many high-cost coastal markets have relatively few listings at that price point.

National housing inventory currently exceeds one million active listings. A significant share of that inventory remains below $250,000, although affordability varies dramatically by region.

The states with the largest total housing inventories are generally Texas and Florida, largely because they have some of the nation's largest populations, housing stocks, and numbers of annual real estate transactions.

This means a buyer searching for a house near the inflation-adjusted 1975 price is far more likely to find options in Texas than in California, and more likely to find options in smaller Midwestern markets than in coastal metropolitan areas.

To give a real-life example of this point, I recently searched how many homes were currently listed for sale across the entire state of Texas for less than $236,505 in early 2026. There were more than 83,000 results. But I dug a little deeper to see if I could find housing at this price within commuting distance of some of the highest priced real estate markets in America.

Buyers can certainly find houses at this price point in these markets; they just don't tend to live in the most popular parts of town. Here are some examples:

San Francisco Bay Area

Buyers can access all or portions of the following counties within a 45-mile radius of downtown San Francisco:

- Solano County

- Contra Costa County
- Eastern Portions of Alameda County
- Portions of Sonoma County

At any given moment, there are often dozens to hundreds of homes listed for less than $236,505 within this broader region. They mostly consist of condos, manufactured homes, senior-community properties, fixer-uppers, and small homes located in very outlying communities.

Examples of move-in ready detached homes in highly desirable job centers located within 45 miles of SF are few and far between.

Seattle

Buyers searching for housing near Seattle can access:

- Pierce County
- Snohomish County
- Parts of Kitsap County

Within 45 miles of downtown Seattle, there will usually be several hundred listings under $236,505. Most of these are condos, manufactured homes, fixer-uppers, or located far away from job centers.

Boston

Buyers living near Boston have access to:

- Southern New Hampshire
- Worcester County
- Portions of Southeastern Massachusetts

Buying within 45 miles of Boston will usually yield dozens, if not hundreds of homes under $236,505. However, the bulk of these are not detached single-family homes located in typical suburban neighborhoods buyers are looking for. They are often condos, older homes, or located far away from job centers.

Washington, D.C.

Buyers near Washington D.C. have access to:

- Frederick County Maryland
- Charles County Maryland
- Parts of West Virginia
- Areas of Virginia outside the popular inner suburbs

Searching within 45 miles of D.C. will usually turn up several hundred homes priced under $236,505. These tend to be townhomes, condos, or detached homes that need renovations.

Los Angeles

Los Angeles is tough, but keep in mind you can reach:

- Parts of Riverside County
- San Bernardino County
- High Desert communities

If you search far enough from Los Angeles, there are hundreds of homes under $236,505. Of course, these are typically manufactured homes, small condos, fixer-uppers or far away from major job centers.

No matter how high prices climb in the hottest markets, there will almost always be homes listed for the inflation-adjusted equivalent of what the median home cost back in 1975. The question is where those homes are located and what they look like:

- Smaller
- Farther from major employment centers
- Older
- Less updated
- Different property types

A median-priced home in 1975 was much closer to where new and future jobs were being created. Today, the inflation-adjusted equivalent is far more likely to be found on the outskirts of expensive metros instead of inside them. It moved away from the jobs

Again, it's not necessarily true that the 1975 house no longer exists.

Rather, the 1975 priced house likely moved farther away from the major employment centers.

But it sure is difficult to find a modest, move-in ready home in a desirable location near today' job centers at the inflation adjusted equivalent of what the median home sold for back in 1975.

There are certainly exceptions. But outside of those niches, buyers who need to live near today's job centers are required to buy homes that cost significantly more than $236,505.

How to Solve the Housing Crisis

Instead of shifting blame and arguing about who is responsible for the housing "crisis", we should be searching farther and working harder to find solutions that meet today' s unique needs.

Homes Have Improved

Many of the houses being compared between generations aren't the same product.

Let's go back to our 1975 example. The typical family may have been able to buy a modest ranch home for $39,300. They likely lasted in that home for 30+ years and took advantage of every opportunity to improve that house.

By 2025, their once modest ranch may now feature:

- Modern windows
- Modern HVAC system
- Updated plumbing
- A renovated kitchen

That's not the same product that was purchased in 1975. It's better.

Buying vs. Affordability Are Not Always the Same Thing

Just because a family can find a house that costs about the same amount as previous generations doesn't automatically mean housing is affordable.

A family could easily buy a house for about the same price as their grandparents, but they may have to:

- Drive farther to work
- Move into an older home with less modern updates
- Move to a different state or region

Simply because a family can purchase a house doesn't automatically mean they will or it's affordable.

Don't Stop Searching

19

Conclusion

The House Was Never Easy

There was never a golden era of homeownership! There was never a time in modern history in America when a median family could purchase a house without sacrifices, risks and financial strain. The sacrifices in 1975 were different than those in 2025 but not necessarily easier.

Boomers have benefited from years of building equity through decades of ownership. This was partly due to neighborhoods that have changed from undesirable to sought after places to live. This helped escalate the values of those homes. It might seem like an unfair advantage for Boomers, but remember that when they bought those homes in those undesirable neighborhoods they took enormous risks. If the neighborhood went in the wrong direction, they could lose.

Comparing Boomers to Millennials is inherently wrong. While I did my best to make the comparisons as closely represent each generation as possible, it is impossible to perfectly account for everything. This would be like comparing a baseball player such as Babe Ruth to Derek Jeter. They played in different eras, faced different competitors and played in different conditions (better fields, more technology and so on).

Comparing different baseball players who played in different eras is hard enough but we are also comparing Millennials who are in the 3rd inning of that baseball game to Boomers who are in the 8th or 9th innings.

Thirty years from now Millennials will have all the assets and it will be Gen Alpha complaining that the Millennials are hoarding all the assets making it harder for them to buy a home and get ahead in life. This is the one constant in life, the current generation blaming the older generations for their hardships. The truth is, every generation has had hardships and every future generation will have hardships that we can't even imagine. This is why it is so important to try and account for these differences in the data when we can.

There are some key areas where we can get a more accurate comparison. This is why the five variables mentioned throughout this book are important. They are used to help us create a common standard.

So what does the data say? Let's look specifically if a median house in 1975 was more or less expensive that a median home in 2025 when we factor in some important variables:

- **Inflation** - the $39,300 home in 1975 is $236,505 in 2025 dollars
- **Square Footage** - 1,500 square foot median home in 1975 to a 1,950 square foot median home in 2025. (30% larger)

Just looking at only these two variables a median 1975 home is equivalent to $307,457. This is how we got this amount:

- $236,505 (inflation adjusted price) x 1.30 (sq ft adjustment) = **$307,457**

A median home in 2025 was $416,00 and the inflation and square footage adjusted price of a 1975 of $307,457. If these were the only two variables to determine if a home in 1975 is more or less expensive than one in 2025, then we would say a median home in 2025 was more expensive. But these are not the only variables that affect affordability.

Our next variable is mortgage interest rates. Let's assume a 20% down payment, 30 year fixed term and only comparing principle and interest for the specific mortgage interest rate in that year.

- **1975** - $307,457 (inflation + sq ft adjusted) median home, $61,491 down payment, 9% interest rate, monthly PI payment - **$1,979**
- **2025** - $416,000 median home, $83,200 down payment, 6.8% interest rate, monthly PI payment - **$2,170**

Based on just these variables a home in 2025 was more expensive than a home in 1975. It is important to note that the difference is very minimal. Now let's continue with our other variables.

Income itself may not have a direct effect on house prices, but it does affect the market as a whole. As incomes increase, the demand for bigger, nicer homes increases right along with those incomes. This is known as "income creep". The more you make, the more you spend. Incomes have increased higher than the rate of inflation in the period between 1975 and 2025.

- **1975** Household Income was $11,800/year (**$71,011** in 2025 dollar)
- **2025** Household Income was **$83,730**/year

This means that when we factor in 2025 median household income of $83,730 a year to the inflation adjusted median household income from 1975 of $71,011 a year, we see that the 2025 income is higher. Millennials had about 18% more household income than Boomers had at their age. This means Millennial have more earnings available to buy a comparable house.

- $83,730 - $71,011 = $12,719 ÷ $71,011 = **18%**

Having more income is always nice but it is meaningless if everything you want to buy goes up in price at the same rate or a higher rate than your income. While incomes have outpaced inflation on a "basket of goods" measured by the Consumer Price Index, when it comes to house prices, this has not been the case.

Another key data point in determining home affordability is the debt-to-income ratio. In 1975, a household making a median income of $11,800/year had a debt-to-income ratio of 3.37 times their income if they purchased a median house. In 2025, the debt-to-income ratio had grown to 4.97 times their median income. Simply put, it would take a Millennial in 2025 almost 5 years of their total income before taxes and deductions to purchase a median house while it only took a Boomer in 1975 almost 3 and ½ years.

When Millennials talk about houses being more unaffordable, this is the reason they feel this way. The size, condition and location of the house is not on the forefront of their minds. This is the major factor that dominates their reasoning for their claim that houses are unaffordable.

The other dominating factor in the housing debate is student loan debt. This was rare for the Boomers but common for Millennials. That $400/month average student loan payment has contributed to delaying first-time homebuyers from purchasing their first home. This delay affected not just their ability to purchase a house but also their ability to start building equity sooner.

Other contributing factors in this housing affordability debate are optional luxuries that have become standard expectations. These are things like granite counter tops, central air conditioning, large closets and finished basements. Even if a homebuyer in 2025 was willing to forego these luxuries, they would most likely already be in a house they are about to buy.

Over the past 50 years the cost of regulation is a cost that can't be avoided and has added significantly to the house affordability debate. These costs are also hard to pinpoint as they are usually assessed at the developer level and then passed on to the homebuyer.

Looking closely at all the available data and accounting for common denominators when comparing the different time periods and different products, the results are clear. Boomers didn't have it easier than Millennials in 1975 and Millennials didn't have it easier than the Boomers in 2025.

Each generation had its challenges but on a comparable basis, they are not far off from each other in total. So the next time you find yourself in the middle of this debate, bring facts and not emotion to argue your points.

I hope this information helps you understand this complex subject.

Thanks for reading!

Notes

Chapter One

3 William H. Frey, Brookings Website, "Baby Boomers are Turning 80" January 7, 2026, https://www.brookings.edu/articles/baby-boomers-are-turning-80/

3 Murray L. Weidenbaum, WashU Scholarly Repository, Website, "Government Regulation and the Cost of Housing", December 7, 1977 https://openscholarship.wustl.edu/cgi/viewcontent.cgi?article=1074&context=mlw_papers

3 Hailey Phelps, Federal Reserve Bank of Richmond, Website, "When Interstates Paved the Way", Febuary 8, 2026, https://www.richmondfed.org/publications/research/econ_focus/2021/q2-3/economic_history

4 Melanie Hanson, Initiative, Website, "Average Student Loan Payment", March 15, 2026, EducationData.org

4 National Center fro Education Statistics, Website, "Digest of Education Statistics", March 15, 2026, https://nces.ed.gov/

5 Federal Reserve Bank of Cleveland, Website, "Inflation Charting", May 2, 2026, https://www.clevelandfed.org/center-for-inflation-research/inflation-charting

6 Freddie Mac, Website, Primary Mortgage Market Survey (PMMS), June 4, 2026, https://www.freddiemac.com/pmms/docs/historicalweeklydata.xlsx

8 Mousumi Sarkar, Freddie Mac, Website, "How American Homes Vary By the Year They Were Built", june 01 2011, https://www.freddiemac.com/pmms/docs/historicalweeklydata.xlsx

Chapter Two

14 FRED (Federal Reserve Bank of St.Louis), Website, Median Sales Price of Houses Sold for the United States (MSPUS), May 5, 2026, https://fred.stlouisfed.org/

15 Bureau of Labor & Statistics, Website, CPI Calculator, Febuary 8, 2026, https://www.bls.gov/

16 Bureau of Labor & Statistics, Website, "Basket of Goods", Febuary 8, 2026, https://www.bls.gov/cpi/questions-and-answers.htm

17 Bureau of Labor & Statistics, Website, "Hedonic Quality Adjustment", March 14, 2026, https://www.bls.gov/cpi/quality-adjustment/hedonic-price-adjustment-techniques.htm

19 JD Power, Website, Research Car Prices, March 14, 2026, https://www.jdpower.com/cars/1980/cadillac/deville/2-door-coupe

20 Realtor.com, Website, "High Mortgage Rates Are Driving Buyers Toward All-Cash Home Purchases", December 22, 2025, https://www.realtor.com/news/trends/mortgage-rates-cash-home-purchases-december-2025/

20 Mortgagecalculator.org, Website, mortgage calculator, Febuary 8, 2026, https://www.mortgagecalculator.org/

21 FRED, Website, "Real Median Household Income in the United States", September 9,2025, https://fred.stlouisfed.org/series/MEHOINUSA672N

22 Capital One, Website, "What's the median household income in the US?", September 21, 2023, https://www.capitalone.com/learn-grow/money-management/average-household-income/

24 Joel Anderson, Yahoo Finance, "What the Average home price today could buy the year you were born", June 18, 2021, https://finance.yahoo.com/news/average-home-price-today-could-190000610.html

24. Farm Bureau Financial Services, Website, "Homes Through the decades", Decemeber 12, 2016, https://www.fbfs.com/learning-center/homes-through-the-decades

24. FRED, Website, "Housing Inventory: Median Home Size in Square Feet in the United States (MEDSQUFEEUS)", July 3, 2026, https://fred.stlouisfed.org/series/MEDSQUFEEUS

25 NAR, Website, "2025 Profile of Homebuyers and sellers", https://www.rirealtors.org/clientuploads/documents/NAR/Homebuyers_and_sellers_trend_2025.pdf

Chapter Three

27 Macrotrends.net, Website, "U.S. House Price Index (1975-2026)", March 1, 2026, https://www.macrotrends.net/3072/us-house-price-index

27 FRED, Website, "Median Sales Price of Houses Sold for the United States (MSPUS)", May 6, 2026, https://fred.stlouisfed.org/series/MSPUS

28 Jessica Lautz, NAR, Website, "Tackling Home Financing and Down Payment Misconceptions", June 30,2025, https://www.nar.realtor/news

/economists-outlook/tackling-home-financing-and-down-payment-misconceptions

29 CFPB, Website, "What is private mortgage insurance?", August 28,2023, https://www.consumerfinance.gov/

31 Wells Fargo, Website, "What is private mortgage insurance (PMI)?", May 8, 2026, https://www.wellsfargo.com/

33 Mortgagecalculator.org, Website, mortgage calculator, Febuary 22, 2026, https://www.mortgagecalculator.org/

Chapter Four

36 Freddie Mac, Website, Primary Mortgage Market Survey, June 4, 2026, https://www.freddiemac.com/pmms?gad_source=1&gad_campaignid=23396332682&gbraid=0AAAAA-zPkSpYTkAmv8DjKfb9WGj_-AEmw&gclid=Cj0KCQjwg5zTBhCLARIsAP2AFU75T-dXrAVQFttWBwP7YihxzQ2M3GnGnXUbTiF4UT5Yd_n-Fsc528IaAkhOEALw_wcB

36 FRED, Website, "Federal Reserve Bank of St. Louis", June 4, 2026, https://fred.stlouisfed.org/

38 Ashley Kilroy, Rocket Mortgage, Website, "What is a good debt-to-income ratio?", April 25, 2024, https://www.rocketmortgage.com/learn/what-is-a-good-debt-to-income-ratio

39 FRED, Website, "Real Median Household Income in the United States", September 9,2025, https://www.mortgagecalculator.org/

39 Freddie Mac, Website, " Primary Mortgage Market Survey (PMMS)", June 4, 2026, https://www.freddiemac.com/pmms/docs/historicalweeklydata.xlsx

41 U.S. Census Bureau, Website, " Historical Income Tables: Household", https://www.census.gov/data/tables/time-series/demo/income-poverty/historical-income-households.html

42 Freddie Mac , Website, " Primary Mortgage Market Survey (PMMS)", June 4, 2026, https://www.freddiemac.com/pmms

Chapter Five

44 FRED, Website, " Real Median Household Income in the United States", September 9,2025, https://www.mortgagecalculator.org/

45 HOWARD HAYGHE, Bureau of Labor & Statistics, Website, "Husbands and wives as earners", https://www.bls.gov/opub/mlr/1981/02/art5full.pdf?

46 Will Freeland, Tax Foundation, Website, "Nonpayers of Federal Taxes and Net Beneficiaries of Federal Spending", September 18,2012, https://taxfoundation.org/blog/nonpayers-federal-taxes-and-net-beneficiaries-federal-spending/

47 Bureau of Labor & Statistics, Website, "TED: The Economic Daily "Wives' earnings as a percentage of family income, 1970–2011", June 2, 2014, https://www.bls.gov/opub/ted/2014/ted_20140602.htm

48 Richard Fry, Pew Research Center, Website, "In a Growing Share of U.S. Marriages, Husbands and Wives Earn About the Same", April 13, 2023, https://www.pewresearch.org/social-trends/2023/04/13/in-a-growing-share-of-u-s-marriages-husbands-and-wives-earn-about-the-same/

50 U.S. Census Bureau, "QuickFacts San Francisco", July 30, 2026, https://www.census.gov/quickfacts/fact/table/sanfranciscocountycalifornia,sanfranciscocitycalifornia/INC110224

50 U.S. Census Bureau, "QuickFacts Dayton, OH", July 30, 2026, https://www.census.gov/quickfacts/fact/table/daytoncityohio/INC110224

52 U.S. Census Bureau, "QuickFacts Hollywood, FL", July 30, 2026, https://www.census.gov/quickfacts/fact/table/hollywoodcityflorida/PST045225

52 U.S. Census Bureau, "QuickFacts Lancaster, PA", July 30, 2026, https://www.census.gov/quickfacts/fact/table/lancastercitypennsylvania/PST045225

52 U.S. Census Bureau, "QuickFacts Atlanta, GA", July 30, 2026, https://www.census.gov/quickfacts/fact/table/atlantacitygeorgia/INC110224

Chapter Six

57 NAHB, Website, https://www.nahb.org/, July 30, 2026 https://www.nahb.org/search#q=do%20i%20have%20to%20build%20roads%20if%20i%20build%20a%20new%20development&tab=all

57 Campbell Property Management, Website, "Who Really owns the roads? When public infrastructure becomes a private burden", February 9, 2026, https://www.campbellpropertymanagement.com/blog/who-really-owns-the-road-when-public-infrastructure-becomes-a-private-burden

59 U.S. Census Bureau, Website, "Characteristics of housing", https://www2.census.gov/library/publications/1997/compendia/statab/117ed/tables/construc.pdf

Chapter Seven

62 Emily Koochel, Emoneyadvisor.com, Website, "How to talk about lifestyle creep with clients", September 8, 2022, https://emoneyadvisor.com/blog/how-to-talk-about-lifestyle-creep-with-clients/

63 HUD, Website, "Federal Influence on Building Codes Through Housing Finance", https://www.huduser.gov/portal/pdredge/pdr-edge-housingat250-article-061126.html

64. U.S. Census Bureau, Website, "Annual Housing Survey: 1975 Part A General Housing Characteristics", https://www2.census.gov/prod2/ahsscan/h150-75a.pdf

65 Nerdwallet.com, Website, "Cost to install central air in 2026", October 1, 2025, https://www.nerdwallet.com/home-ownership/home-improvement/learn/cost-to-install-central-air

69 Reviews.com, Website, "Median spending 2025: how much are Americans paying to stay connected?", https://www.reviews.org/internet-service/cost-of-internet-streaming-and-cell-phone-bills/

72 Abigal Fagan, Psychologytoday.com, Website, "Hedonic Treadmill", November 12, 2025, https://www.psychologytoday.com/us/basics/hedonic-treadmill

Chapter Nine

81 NAHB, Website, "Regulatory costs jump 40% in five years, add $131,734 to New home prices", https://www.nahb.org/news-and-economics/press-releases/2026/06/regulatory-costs-jump-40-in-five-years-add-131734-to-new-home-prices

81 Withpuley, Website, "The history of permitting, why it's slow, and how we fix it", https://www.withpulley.com/resources/permitting-how-we-got-here-and-how-to-move forward

81 apa.gov, Website, "What is the National Environmental Policy Act?", https://www.epa.gov/nepa/what-national-environmental-policy-act

82 gfoa.org, Website, "Impact Fees", https://www.gfoa.org/materials/impact-fees

Chapter Ten

87 FRED , Website, "Federal Reserve Bank of St. Louis", https://fred.stlouisfed.org/series/POPTHM

87 Earth, Website, "The East-West divide: understanding why 80% of Americans call the east home", https://vocal.media/earth/the-east-west-divide-understanding-why-80-of-americans-call-the-east-home

88 U.S. Census Bureau, Website, "Historical Households Tables", https://www.census.gov/data/tables/time-series/demo/families/households.html

89 U.S. Census Bureau, Website, "General housing characteristics", https://www2.census.gov/prod2/ahsscan/h150-75a.pdf

91 Robslink.com, Website, "Divorce Rate in the US", https://robslink.com/SAS/democd80/us_divorce_and_marriage.htm

91. National Center for Health Statistics, Website, "Marriage and divorce", https://www.cdc.gov/nchs/fastats/marriage-divorce.htm

92 CATO, Website, "First-time homebuyer crisis: fact or fiction?", https://www.cato.org/blog/first-time-homebuyer-crisis-fact-or-fiction

Chapter Eleven

94 ReSub, Website, "Subscription Spending Statistics (2026): What the Data Shows", March 3, 2026, https://resubs.app/resources/subscription-spending-statistics

95 The Christian Science Monitor, Website, "Cable TV faces new competition in multichannel plan", August 10, 1982, https://www.csmonitor.com/1982/0810/081029.html

97 Alexa Figliuolo, CloudKitchens, Website, "The US Food Delivery Market: Growth Data and Opportunities", April 3, 2025, https://cloudkitchens.com/blog/food-delivery-statistics-and-opportunities

97 Fidelity, Website, "What is the S&P 500 average return?", March 6, 2026, https://www.fidelity.com/learning-center/trading-investing/sp-500-average-return

103 Fidelity, Website, "What is the S&P 500 average return?", March 6, 2026, https://www.fidelity.com/learning-center/trading-investing/sp-500-average-return

104 CQ Press, Website, "Federal housing Administration (FHA) Insurance Program shored up", June 12, 1905, https://library.cqpress.com/cqalmanac/document.php?id=cqal90-1113602#_

105 NAR, Website, "Median percent down payment by first time and repeat buyers 1989-2025", https://www.nar.realtor/news/real-estate-news/nar-2025-profile-of-home-buyers-sellers-reveals-market-extremes

105 Joy Dumandan, Realtor.com, Website, "VA Loans Are Helping Veterans Buy Their First Homes With 0% Down Advantage", November 10, 2025, https://www.realtor.com/news/trends/va-loans-zero-down-payment-veterans-first-home/

106 Down payment Resource, Website, "Down Payment assistance is available", https://downpaymentresource.com/

Chapter Twelve

109 Economyleague.org, Website, "The Big Payoff: Educational Attainment and Estimates of Work-Life Earnings", https://www.economyleague.org/sites/default/files/legacy/3346880195448024 4-the-big-payoff-educational-attainment-and-estimates-of-work-life-earnings.pdf

109 Community College Daily, Website, "DataPoints: Educational Attainment in the U.S.", https://www.ccdaily.com/2025/09/datapoints-educational-attainment-in-the-u-s/

110 Melanie Hanson, Education data initiative, Website, "Average cost of college by year", https://educationdata.org/average-cost-of-college-by-year

111 US News, Website, "Average College Tution in 2025-2026", https://www.usnews.com/education/best-colleges/paying-for-college/articles/paying-for-college-infographic

112 Education data initiative, Website, "Average Monthly Student Loan Payments", https://educationdata.org/average-student-loan-payment

112. Chase, Website, "What is debt to income ratio and why is it important", https://www.chase.com/personal/credit-cards/education/basics/what-is-debt-to-income-ratio-and-why-it-is-important

114 Social Security Administration, Website, "Education and lifetime earnings", https://www.ssa.gov/policy/docs/research-summaries/education-earnings.html

115 PR Newswire, Website, "Today's first-time homebuyers older, more often single", https://www.prnewswire.com/news-releases/todays-first-time-homebuyers-older-more-often-single-300129440.html

116 NAR, Website, "First-time home buyer share falls to historic low of 21% Median age rises to 40", November 4, 2025, https://www.nar.realtor/press-r

eleases/first-time-home-buyer-share-falls-to-historic-low-of-21-median-age-rises-to-40

116 AEI.org, Website, "Medan First-time homebuyers age at 34 years in 2025, Little changed from 2024", February 19, 2026, https://www.aei.org/research-products/report/median-first-time-homebuyer-age-at-34-years-in-2025-little-changed-from-2024/

116 MBA.org, Website, "Chart of the week: median first-time homebuyer age", July 20, 2026, https://newslink.mba.org/servicing-newslink/2026/july/mba-servicing-newslink-tuesday-july-21-2026/chart-of-the-week-median-first-time-homebuyer-age/

118 Albert Einstein, "Compound interest is the eighth wonder of the world. He who understands it, earns it: he who doesn't, pays it"

Chapter Thirteen

123 Sarah Henseler, Rocket Mortgage, Website, "What is house hacking and is it something you should be doing?", May 8, 2026, https://www.rocketmortgage.com/learn/house-hacking

125 US bureau of labor & statistics, BLS.gov, Website, https://www.bls.gov/ooh/media-and-communication/writers-and-authors.htm

126 Every city in the usa, Website, "San Francisco, CA Population 2025", https://www.everycityintheusa.com/cities/san-francisco-ca/

128 Education data initiative, Website, "Average Monthly Student Loan Payments", https://educationdata.org/average-student-loan-payment

Chapter Fourteen

131 Eliza Reiman, Business Insider, Website, "See the ciites where mega-investors own the most single-family homes", January 10, 2026, https://www.businessinsider.com/institutional-investors-single-family-homes-cities-map-2026-1

132 FRED , Website, "Housing inventory estimate: total housing units in the US", https://fred.stlouisfed.org/series/ETOTALUSQ176N

133 FHFA, Website, "U.S. Federal Housing", May 26, 2026, https://www.fhfa.gov/news/news-release/u.s.-house-prices-rise-1.7-percent-year-over-year-up-0.5-percent-quarter-over-quarter

Chapter Fifteen

135 Andrea Riquier, USA today, Website, "No national market anymore: all real estate is local, again", May 27, 2026, https://www.usatoday.com/story/money/personalfinance/real-estate/2026/05/27/national-housing-market-real-estate-local/90258472007/

137 Redfin, Website, "San Francisco, CA Housing Market", https://www.redfin.com/city/17151/CA/San-Francisco/housing-market

138 Zillow, Website, "median house cost in rural Kansas", https://www.zillow.com/home-values/23/ks/

Chapter Sixteen

142 Investopedia, Website, unraveling the 2008 stock market crash: casuses and aftermath, https://www.investopedia.com/articles/economics/09/subprime-market-2008.asp

143 Bankrate, Website, "Mortgage rate history: 1972 to 2026", https://www.bankrate.com/mortgages/historical-mortgage-rates/

144 Julia kagan, Investopedia, Website, "Understanding NINJA Loans: Risks, Impact, and current status", May 14, 2026, https://www.investopedia.com/terms/n/ninja-loan.asp

146 Julia Falcon, housing wire, "Here's how many homes were built in the last decade", January 6, 2026, https://www.housingwire.com/articles/heres-how-many-homes-were-built-in-the-last-decade/

147 Rose Quint, Eye on housing, "US governemnet: Number of builders declined 50% between 2007 and 2012", September 9, 2026, https://eyeonhousing.org/2015/09/us-government-number-of-builders-declined-50-between-2007-and-2012/

150 Federal Reserve Bank of Cleveland, Website, "Household Formation and the Great Recession", August 23, 2012, https://www.clevelandfed.org/publications/economic-commentary/2012/ec-201212-household-formation-and-the-great-recession

Chapter Seventeen

155 Bankrate, Website, "Mortgage rate history: 1972 to 2026", https://www.bankrate.com/mortgages/historical-mortgage-rates/

157 Macrotrends.net, Website, "Median house cost In Cleveland 1975", macrotrends.net/4291/cleveland-area-home-price-index

157 U.S. Census Bureau, Website, "Median Home Values: Un adjusted all states", https://www2.census.gov/programs-surveys/decennial/tables/time-series/coh-values/values-unadj.txt

158 Redfin, Website, "2025 Housing market Year in Review: Is There Anybody Out There?", July 30, 2025, https://www.redfin.com/blog/housing-market-year-in-review-2025/

160 Bureau of Labor & Statistics, Website, CPI Calculator, bls.gov

161 U.S. Census Bureau, Website, "General housing characteristics", https://www2.census.gov/prod2/ahsscan/h150-75a.pdf

161 U.S. Census Bureau, Website, "American Housing Survey (AHS)", https://www.census.gov/programs-surveys/ahs.html

167 Jake Krimmel, Realtor.com, Website, "November 2025 Monthly Housing Market Trends Report", December 8, 2026, https://www.realtor.com/research/november-2025-data/

Chapter Eighteen

174 Realtor.com, Website, "Places Across the US Where You can still buy a home for $300k or less", https://www.realtor.com/news/trends/affordable-cities-to-buy-home-under-300000/

About the Author

James W. Lamprey is a researcher and writer with a deep interest in housing affordability, personal finance, and economic decision-making. He studied business, finance, and economics during his undergraduate education, building a strong foundation in the forces that shape markets, household budgets, and long-term wealth creation. He later pursued graduate studies focused on investing through **Johns Hopkins Carey Business School**, further expanding his understanding of capital markets, real estate, and financial strategy.

James also brings practical industry experience to his work. In the early 2000s, he was a licensed Realtor in the Washington, D.C. area, giving him firsthand exposure to housing markets, mortgage dynamics, and the challenges families face when trying to buy a home. He also held investment industry certifications including the **NASD Series 6** and **Series 63**, reflecting his background in financial products and investor education.

Throughout his career, he has been passionate about helping people better understand their financial options. He believes that clear information, honest analysis, and historical perspective can empower ordinary people to make smarter decisions about housing, debt, investing, and wealth building.

Through his writing, James aims to turn complex economic topics into practical knowledge that can benefit the widest possible audience.

You can connect with me on:

https://boomersvsmillennials.com

https://www.facebook.com/TheAmericanHomebuyer

Subscribe to my newsletter:

https://magic.beehiiv.com/v1/7013d980-ee62-4389-84d5-d39329c4f1e0?email=%7B%7Bemail%7D%7D